the soccer method

DEFENDING

Henk Mariman

**Library of Congress
Cataloging - in - Publication Data**

the Soccer Method
Book 4 - Defending
by Henk Mariman

ISBN-13: 978-1-59164-106-3
ISBN-10: 1-59164-106-3
Library of Congress Control Number: 2006903029
© 2006

Editing
Bryan R. Beaver

Translation from Dutch
Dave Brandt

Printed by
Data Reproductions
Auburn, Michigan

Reedswain Publishing
562 Ridge Road
Spring City, PA 19475
www. reedswain.com
info@reedswain.com

Contents

Introduction

The coaching of young soccer players is based primarily on having possession of the ball. Clearly the players must learn how to play when their team has the ball. However, they must also learn about playing when the opposition has possession. Ultimately they must be able to perform in real games, and in real games their team will not always have the ball.

Coaching for the "opposing team in possession" situation must be placed in the correct context. Aims such as closing down the player in possession as a means of influencing the result of the game must not be overemphasized. An excessive focus on pressing, at the expense of retaining possession, results in "ping pong" soccer. Both sides lose possession too often due to the extreme pressure on the ball, and technique takes a back seat to power play with lots of tackles. This does not promote the development of soccer skills.

Nevertheless, taking account of a healthy balance between the "in possession" and "opposition in possession" situations, targeted pressing can be a useful aim. The fact that all the players are in one half and pressure is exerted on the ball means that space is in short supply. Greater demands are therefore made on the team in possession.

"Defending" is then also a key element. In view of the significance of the aspect "opposition in possession," young players of all ages should be confronted with it. This must be done properly.

THE CONTENTS OF THIS BOOK

After reading this book, a coach should be able to incorporate defensive play into his training sessions.

Section 1: All typical aspects of defensive play that need to be worked on ("work items") are collected here. I have distilled the most important work items from the numerous soccer matches I have watched between teams of young players.

In **section 2**, I define the tasks and functions of the total team, the lines of the team (defense, midfield, attack) and the specific positions (based on a 1-3-4-3 team formation).

In **section 3**, I describe all the aims associated with defensive play. These aims are aligned to the chosen playing system (see the Soccer Manual). There are explanations of the typical aspects that need to be worked on, especially closing down/defending in the opposition's half.

Section 4 is about the different principles, such as "squeezing", forcing opponents inside or toward the flank, etc.

Section 5 deals with 3 types of 1v1 situation: "opponent in front," "opponent alongside," and "opponent behind." Each situation has its own specific coaching points. We also look at how to defend against crosses.

Coaches of young soccer players can use a 3-man defense reinforced by a defensive midfielder. The defensive midfielder has a number of tasks, as described in **section 6**.

Work Items

WORK ITEMS

In recent years I have watched a lot of youth soccer matches at various levels. I have identified the most important aspects of play when the opposing team has possession.

The opposing team passes the ball around in its own half and is able to play the ball forward. The defending team's players do not push toward the flank where the ball is.

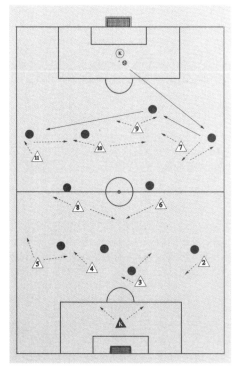

The players must adjust their position in relation to the position of the ball and their direct opponent.

The lines are too far apart

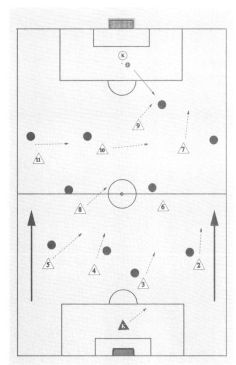

The distance between the lines is too great. This means that the opposing team can find openings to work the ball forward.

Sometimes the defenders push forward well but the midfielders hang back too far.

This means that there is too much space between the attackers and the midfielders, which the opposing team can exploit to work the ball forward.

Some of the players are not in position

The players must combine to put pressure on the ball.

The attackers allow themselves to be by-passed too easily.

The attackers are the first line of defense. It is essential that they close down the player in possession effectively.

The players do not chase the ball energetically enough

If too little pressure is exerted on the opposing player, who is therefore not forced to make use of his soccer insight or technique, there is no point in exerting pressure at all.

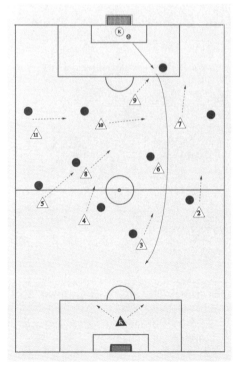

When we exert pressure in the opposing team's half, we inevitably leave space behind the backs of the defenders. It is important that the goalkeeper guards this space.

The point is to win the ball, not to cause loss of possession.

The distance between the defenders and midfielders is too great.

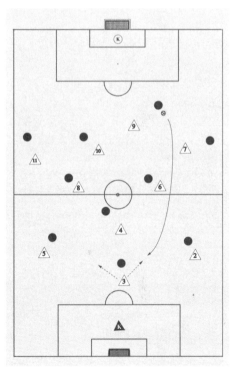

If too much space is left between the defenders and the midfielders, the opposing team can exploit this to work the ball forward. The attacker has more freedom of movement and the ball can easily be passed to him.

The attackers neglect their defensive duties

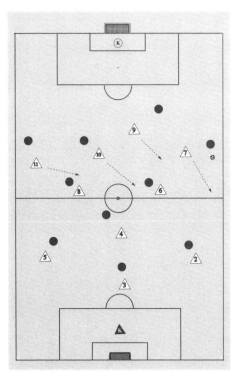

The central defender allows himself to be drawn out of position

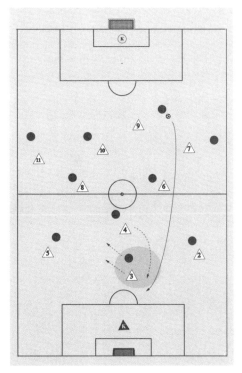

"When your team loses possession, you can avoid having to run back thirty yards after the ball by taking just one step. As a winger you can position yourself so that the back cannot go forward and, secondly, so that he cannot receive the ball.."

Johan Cruyff

If the central defender follows the opposing player's run, he leaves space in the center of the defense. This makes the defense vulnerable to advancing midfielders.

Too much space is left on the flank where the ball is

The defenders fail to cover the center sufficiently

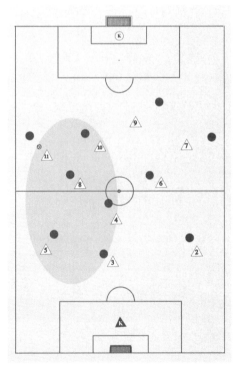

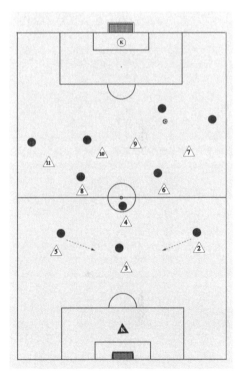

The defending team's players must mark their opponents very closely.

It is important that the 3 defenders work well together and cover the center very efficiently.

The task of winning the ball is not complete until a teammate has the ball!

The players fail to cover each other

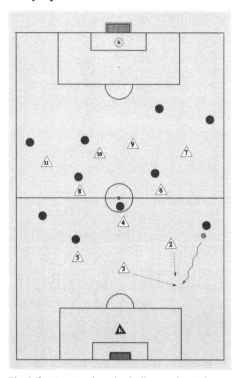

The left winger takes the ball past the right
back (2), so the central defender (3) moves
across to block the winger. The right back fails
to move into the center to take over the position vacated by the central defender.

Tasks and functions

We have chosen a 1-3-4-3 system, to which we have linked a way of playing. Within each system and the associated way of playing, there are tasks and functions for the team as a whole, the lines (defense, midfield, attack) and the individual positions. The tasks and functions in this description are totally oriented to the development of young soccer players.

Age plays a key role here. The tasks and functions differ for each age group. The tasks and functions described here are aimed at 14 to 18-year-olds. Coaches of other age groups can integrate these tasks and functions without inhibiting the individuality of their own players.

By describing the tasks and functions, I am not putting the players in a straightjacket. Youth soccer should not be stereotyped. Assigning tasks to young players that they must carry out when the opposing team is in possession of the ball must not limit them. The tasks and functions described here are more a framework for the coach than a target to be achieved.

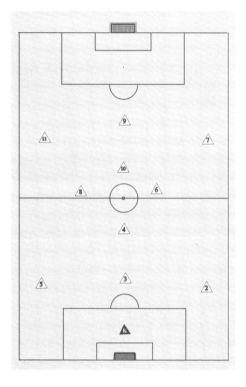

TASKS FOR THE WHOLE TEAM (DEFENDING)

- The objective is to win the ball back as soon as possible.
- Try to defend as far away from your goal as possible.
- Make the playing area as small as possible (in length and width).
- The player with the ball must be marked closely.
- Choose the right moment to pressure the opposing players.
- Don't always chase at the same speed.
- Trigger a chain reaction – force the opposing player to make a bad pass.
- Be compact – stay close together.

TASKS FOR THE INDIVIDUAL LINES (DEFENDING)

Defensive line
- Support the other lines. Each time the opposition wins the ball, the defenders must move up in support.
- The closer you are to your own goal, the more closely you must mark the opposing players.
- Always try to have one man more than the opposition.
- Don't commit unnecessary fouls.
- Push toward the flank where the ball is.
- Be aware of where your teammates are.

Midfield line
- Don't neglect your defensive duties. When too many midfielders are in front of the ball, the midfield is vulnerable.

- Communicate.
- Support the attackers.
- Push toward the flank where the ball is.
- Don't "sell yourself" too quickly. Avoid diving in or acting too impulsively.

Attacking line
- Make sure the team is in position.
- Don't chase opposing players on your own.
- Try to prevent the opposing players from passing the ball forward.
- Choose the right moment to challenge for the ball.
- Cooperate to close down the player in possession.

TASKS PER POSITION (DEFENDING)

Goalkeeper (1)
- Try to intercept the ball as soon as possible.
- The priority is to avoid conceding a goal.
- Adjust your position relative to the positions of the defenders.
- "Read" the opposing team's build-up play.
- Remain active, maintain your concentration.
- Give directions to your defenders, especially with regard to "squeezing" and moving up in support.

Central Defender (3)
- The priority is to avoid conceding a goal.
- Give directions to the other defenders.

- Be aware of the overall situation.
- Provide sufficient cover to cope with a long forward pass from the opposition.
- Choose the right moment to move back to fall back and cover the space behind the defensive line.
- Make sure the players are not too far apart from each other.
- Use your strength when challenging for the ball.

Defensive Midfielder (4)
- Make sure the team maintains its defensive organization.
- Use your strength when challenging for the ball.
- Don't go too far forward. Stay in contact with the central defender.
- Depending on the situation, play in front of or in the defensive line.
  - In front of the defensive line
    If the defensive midfielder plays in front of the defense, he is responsible for picking up the attacking midfielder of the opposing team.
  - In the defensive line
    If an opponent infiltrates through the center, or if the central defender needs help.

Right and Left Backs (2 and 5)
- The priority is to avoid conceding a goal.
- The closer you are to the ball, the closer the marking.
- Position yourself between your opponent and the goal.
- Move inside and provide cover when the ball is on the other flank.
- Push up in support.
- Stay concentrated in 1v1 situations. Use your weight when you challenge for the ball.
- Communicate with the players in front of you.

Midfielders (6 and 8)
- Choose the right moment to exert pressure on the ball.
- Remember your defensive duties. Ensure that you are behind the ball.
- Join in when pressure is exerted on the ball.
- Make sure that the opposing player has no opportunities to escape.
- Make sure there is always a good defensive balance in midfield. Don't play too far forward.
- Move across to provide cover for the other midfielder when the ball is on the other flank.

- Communicate with the players in front of you.
- Mark your opponent closely when the ball is on your flank.
- Push up in support.

Withdrawn Striker (10)
- Move across toward the flank where the ball is.
- Close down the opposing player's escape routes.
- Try to anticipate the striker's runs.
- Don't allow the opposing team to play the ball past you too easily.
- Choose the right moment to pressure your opponent.

Striker (9)
- Force the opposing player in possession toward the flank.
- Choose the right moment to challenge for the ball.
- Force your opponent to use his weaker foot.
- Don't allow the opposing team to play the ball past you too easily.
- Close down the opposing player's escape routes.
- Combine with teammates to close down the opposing players.

Wingers (7 and 11)
- Exert pressure on your opponent.
- Don't allow the opposing team to play the ball past you too easily.
- Move inside when the ball is on the other flank.
- Prevent the opposing players from playing the ball forward.
- Close down the opposing player's escape routes.

The aims of the game

CLOSING DOWN/DEFENDING

The game of soccer can be broken down into 3 situations: own team in possession, opposing team in possession, and change of possession. The "opposing team in possession" phase can in turn be broken down into 3 phases:

- **1st aim:** To close down/defend in order to win possession and score (defending in the opposing team's half).
- **2nd aim:** To close down/defend in order to win possession and attack (defending in and around the center circle).
- **3rd aim:** To close down/defend in order to win possession and build-up a move (defending in own half).

To achieve this, we must describe closing down/defending in detail. In this section I explain the basics of defensive play in a manner that furthers the players' development. I discuss the most common aims and principles of closing down/defending.

The aims of closing down/defending

Aims:
- To intercept the ball as soon as possible or close down the opposing players to prevent them building up a move.
- To prevent the opposing team from scoring.

By:
- Winning 1v1 challenges.
- Good positional play.
- Choosing the right moment to challenge for the ball.

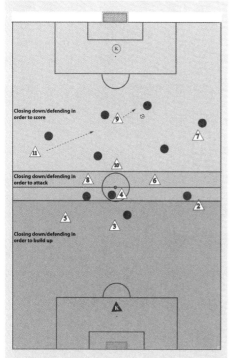

In principle we try to close down the player in possession as quickly as possible to prevent the opposing team from building up a move. Depending on the strength of the opposing team, this can occur in the opposition's half, in and around the center circle or in the team's own half.

The aims of the game must be translated into practice to promote the individual development of the players rather than just to get a result.

The key phases of closing down/defending

The following aspects of closing down and defending are important:

1. Exerting pressure on the ball
- The player closest to the ball exerts pressure.
- The aim is to prevent the ball from being played forward.
- Mark the players with and around the ball very closely.
- Don't allow the opposing team to play the ball past you too easily.

2. Make the playing area as small as possible
- Close down the space around the ball.
- Move infield, pressure the ball and, if necessary, defend zonally.

3. Collective action
- Each player must join in.
- Exert pressure collectively.
- Defend cohesively.

4. Winning the ball
- Wait for the right moment
- No fouls

1st aim: Intense pressing zone

To pressure the opposition and to defend in the opposing team's half in order to win possession and score.

2nd aim: Medium pressing zone

To close down the opposition and to defend in and around the center circle in order to win possession and attack.

3rd aim: Low pressing zone

To close down the opposition and to defend in the team's own half in order to win possession and build-up a move.

The aims of the game

Defending as far away from the team's own goal is a priority in this module. A style of play aimed at regaining possession as soon as possible is good for the players' development. A defensive approach might result in more matches being won, but does little for the players' soccer education. The motto is "Defense is a means to an end, not an end in itself." When the opposing team has the ball, the focus is on the recovery of the ball and rather than loss of possession. Whatever resistance the opposing team offers, the emphasis must always be on winning the ball.

The 3 phases associated with closing down the opposing players and winning the ball are dealt with next.

1st aim
To close down the opposition and defend in order to win possession and score
Intense pressing zone
We try to pen the opposition into its own half for as long as possible.

Aim: *To pen the opposing team in its own half by exerting pressure on the ball, winning possession as soon as possible, and creating chances and scoring by means of efficient build-up play.*

Pressure is immediately exerted to block the opposition's build-up play. The aim is to win the ball and score as quickly as possible. We pen the opposing team in its own half by exerting pressure during the most vulnerable phase of possession, i.e. the build-up. Closing down the opposing players in this way is the first aim when the opposition has possession.

Theory
The best place to exert pressure on the opposing players is on the flank. The opportunities for building up a move are more restricted here, given the proximity of the sideline. In the center the opposing players have more options. The player with the ball can be forced inside or outside.

Option 1: Forcing the player with the ball toward the flank

Example
1. **When the weakest defender has the ball, the striker makes a run and forces him toward the flank.**

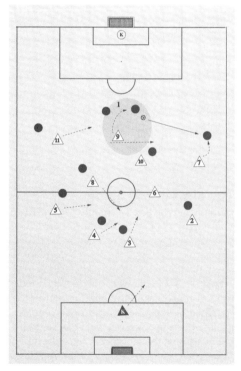

Focusing excessively on defending as far forward as possible can be disadvantageous for the development of players' skills when they are in possession.

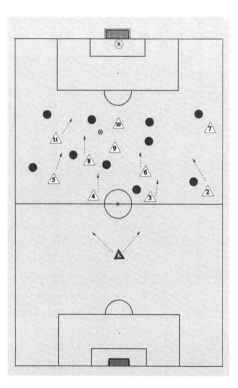

Execution:
- Some coaches tell the central player to give the signal to start. This is out of date. Giving a signal often makes the drill less realistic. It is better to view the moment when the striker starts his run as the start of the drill. If the run is badly executed, the other players can still decide to remain in a block and not to exert pressure.
- The striker forces the central defender, who has the ball, toward the flank.

Diagram 1

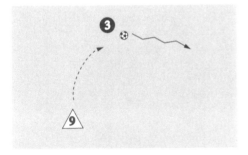

Diagram 2

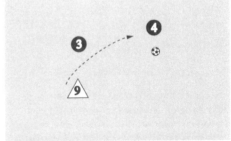

The striker (9) runs diagonally toward the central defender (3), thus exerting pressure. This forces the central defender to move in a certain direction, e.g. toward the flank. Many central defenders are one-footed. Forcing the defender in the direction of his weaker foot increases the chances of winning the ball back. If the opposing team plays with two central defenders, one of them is virtually inaccessible (diagram 2).

"We try to mark all the players, except the weakest defender."

Mick Priest, Manchester United

15

2. The winger forces his opponent inside

Execution:
- When the ball is on the flank, the winger (7) immediately pressures his opponent.
- He angles his run so that his opponent is forced inside.

Forcing the opposing player inside:

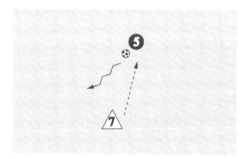

The right winger (7) pressures the left back (5), who is therefore forced to move inside.
The advantages are:
- All the winger's teammates have moved toward the ball. The center of the field is therefore densely populated.
- A left back who moves inside is forced to use his right foot, which increases the chance of losing possession.

> "The easiest way to defend is from inside to outside. Make sure you don't have to chase after your opponent!"
>
> *Herman Vermeulen*

It is important to run straight at the full back, leaving him just a little more space on the inside. If the full back is given too much space on the inside he has more chance of taking the ball past the winger, who will then have to chase after him.

The winger (7) must not stand too far away from the full back. Good timing is an essential aspect of exerting pressure on the ball. The winger must start to run toward the full back at the moment when the ball is passed to him. He should therefore stand relatively close to the full back (about 10 yards away).

3. All the players then push toward the flank where the ball is.

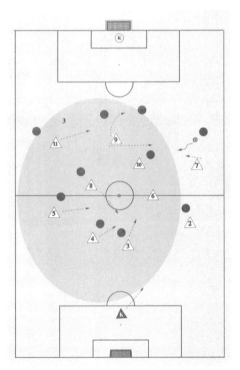

a) The left winger (11) moves inside

The left winger moves inside. In principle, the players on his flank are left free. As a result, a one-man-more situation can be created on the flank where the ball is.

The left winger can:

- Mark the right central defender.

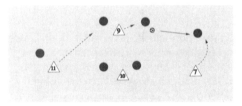

- Or he can mark the right midfielder.

Execution:
- The left winger (11) moves inside.
- The withdrawn striker (10) covers the flank where the ball is.
- The striker (9) covers the center and looks out for a backpass.
- The midfielders (6 and 8) move toward the flank where the ball is and cover the passing lines toward the center.
- The left back (5) moves infield and covers the center.
- The right back (2) marks his opponent closely on the flank where the ball is.
- The central defender (3) and the defensive midfielder (4) mark their opponents closely in the center.
- The right winger (7) pressures the ball.
- The goalkeeper watches out for a long forward pass.

b) Withdrawn striker (10) covers the flank where the ball is

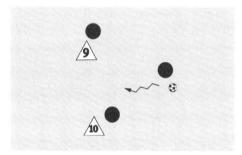 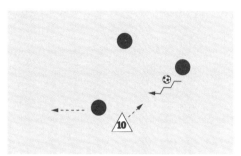

If the opposing team plays with a central midfielder, the withdrawn striker can mark him. If the midfielder moves away, the withdrawn striker does not always have to follow him. Zonal defense, covering the passing line, may be sufficient to isolate the central midfielder if he moves away.

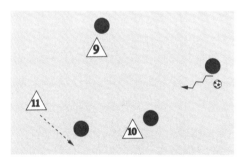

If the opposing team plays with 2 defensive midfielders alongside each other, the withdrawn striker can best mark the defensive midfielder who is closest to the ball. The other midfielder is often inaccessible (the passing line is closed off). The players who have moved infield from the other side of the field (left winger) are nearby and can restrict the escape options.

> "The players must react as soon as the ball is on its way"
>
> *Jos Daerden*

c) Midfielders cover the passing line

Diagram 1

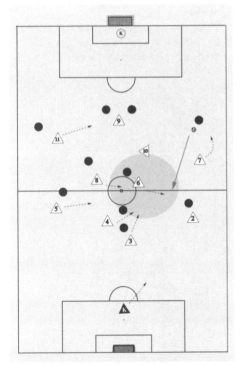

Diagram 2

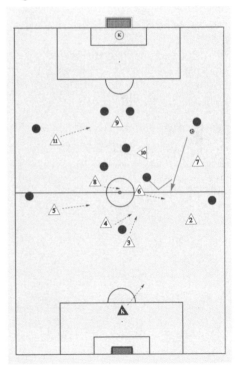

The left midfielder (8) moves infield, covers the right midfielder (6) and marks an opponent. The right midfielder positions himself on the line between the ball and the center. This makes it difficult for the opposition's left back to pass the ball to an attacker (Diagram 1). If there is another opponent in this zone, he stands "in between." Besides covering off the passing line, he ensures that he remains close to his opponent.

General aspects of closing down the opposition:

- Avoid being bypassed.
- Defend to the front; don't run back.
- Tackle only as a last resort.
- Defending is a chain reaction. The third challenger might win the ball.
- Use your weight when you challenge.
- The team's lines must stay close together.
- Mark your opponent closely on the flank where the ball is.
- There is no point is chasing toward the goalkeeper unless you can really put him under pressure.

When should we force an opponent infield?
This depends on your own skills and those of the opposing team.

If the opposing team likes to attack down the flank
Some teams are strong on the flanks. They might have an attacking right or left back, possibly with a strong attacker who often moves out to the flank.

If the opposing player has a weaker foot
A left back with a weak right foot is more vulnerable if he is forced infield.

Option 2: Forcing the opposing player to go outside

Example:
1. When the weakest defender has the ball, the striker (9) runs to challenge him, forcing him toward the flank.

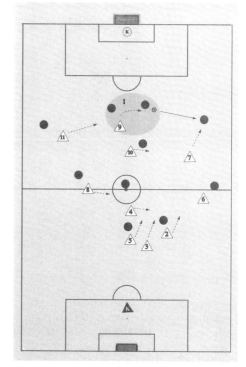

Execution:
- Often a central player gives a signal to exert pressure. However, it is better to see the striker's run as the start signal. If the run is badly timed, the other players can always decide to stay in formation and not exert pressure.
- The striker's run forces the central defender toward the flank.

2. The right winger (7) forces the left back (5) toward the flank

3. All the players then push toward the flank where the ball is.

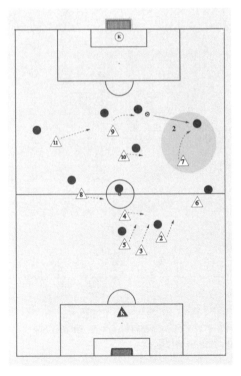

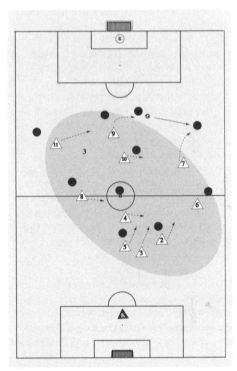

Execution:
- After the ball is played to the full back, the right winger exerts pressure toward the flank. The defender is forced to the outside.
- Here, too, timing is important. The winger must exert pressure as soon as the ball is passed to the full back.

Execution:
- The left winger (11) moves inside.
- The striker (9) covers the center and looks out for a backpass.
- The withdrawn striker (10) covers the flank where the ball is.
- The midfielders (6 and 8) move toward the flank where the ball is.
- The right back (2) and the left back mark their opponents closely.
- The defensive midfielder (4) covers the passing line to the center.
- The central defender (3) covers the right back and the left back.
- The right winger (7) pressures the ball.
- The goalkeeper watches out for a long forward pass.

There are fewer passing options on the flank. The opposing player only has a small corridor in which to play the ball. A pass from the right back to the right winger is very risky and is easy to defend against.

General aspects of closing down the opposition:

- All the players push toward the flank where the ball is.
- The team's lines must stay close together.
- Mark your opponent closely on the flank where the ball is.
- Avoid being bypassed.
- Defend to the front; don't run back.
- Tackle only as a last resort.
- Defending is a chain reaction. The third challenger might win the ball.
- Use your weight.

When should we force an opponent toward the flank?

This depends on your own skills and those of the opposing team. Forcing an opponent toward the flank leaves him the least possible number of options.

When the opposition plays on just one flank

In this situation the opposing player who is in possession must be isolated. In the example, the opposing team plays in a 1-3-5-2 formation. When the player on the flank has the ball, he is forced outside. The team in possession is therefore unable to exploit its numeric superiority in midfield and the chance of losing possession is greater.

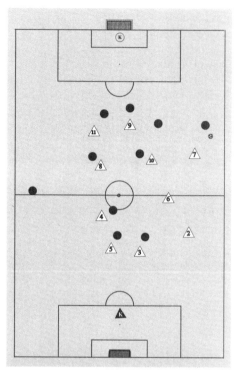

When the opposing team's strengths are mainly in midfield.

If the opposing team has dominant players in midfield, it is best to cut off the passing lines from the flank to the center. The less of the ball these players see, the less dangerous they are.

2nd aim

To close down the opposition and defend in order to win possession and score
In and around the center circle
Medium pressing zone
It is not always possible to play pressure soccer. If you do not succeed in penning the opposing team into its own half, the play might be concentrated around the center circle.

Aim: ***To react quickly to losing possession and thus restore the organizational balance of the team, regain possession and create chances by means of efficient build-up play.***

The team plays a waiting game and takes up positions around the center circle. As a result, there is more space behind the opposing players when possession is regained. This way of playing may be chosen deliberately or it may be imposed by the strength of the opposition.

Theory

Because the opposing team has more time and space to build up its play, it is important to choose the right moment to challenge for the ball. A careless pass, a dangerous square pass or a player's poor control when receiving a pass may offer a chance to win the ball.

If the team decides to leave the opposition's weakest player unmarked, the other opposition players must be marked closely to reduce the options of the player in possession.

After the ball has been won, there is more space behind the opposition players and this makes them vulnerable. The principles of closing down the opposition are similar to those that apply to pressuring the opposition in its own half.

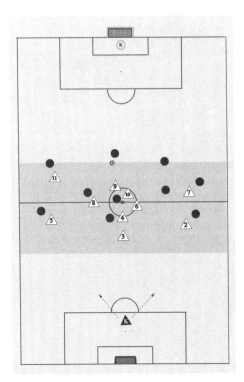

3rd aim

To close down the opposition and defend in order to build up a move
Outside the team's own penalty area
Low pressing zone

Low pressing zone

If the opposing team is very strong, you might come under pressure yourself and your team may find it difficult to escape from this pressure.

Aim: **To regain possession by remaining well organized, and then to push the opposing team back by means of efficient build-up play.**

This third aim may not be a conscious choice – it may be forced on the team by the opposition. Opting for a low pressing zone is too defensive.

Theory

For the older group of players, it is sometimes interesting to focus on the low pressing zone. The ability to defend a 1-0 lead in the final minutes of a hard-fought game is a skill in it-self. Close marking in front of the goal is often a neglected topic in the older age groups. In practice, some talented players do not have the mental strength to handle this. They lack the shrewdness, the will to win and tough-ness required to come out on top. Coaching the low pressure option can contribute to the mental development of the players. Being able to avoid conceding a goal is also part of the game of soccer.

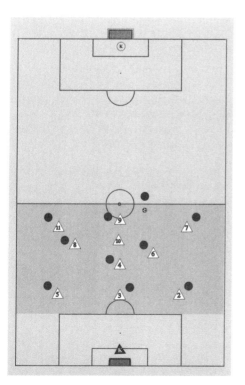

Winning a dropping ball

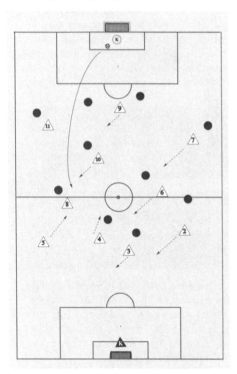

Some goalkeepers choose (consciously or unconsciously) to kick the ball downfield. The player closest to the falling ball challenges for it. The other players close down the space around the ball as efficiently as possible. After the challenge, pressure is exerted on the ball and we try to win possession.

Coaching points:
- The players closest to the ball always challenge (even if they can't win possession).
- Try to intercept the ball from the goalkeeper before it bounces.
- One of the players in the defensive line falls back so that there is less space for the attackers in the final third.
- All the players move toward the half of the field where the goalkeeper has the ball. Even the attackers drop back. The players try to be in their own positions at the moment when the goalkeeper kicks the ball.
- The moment after the challenge for the ball is crucial. The opposing players do not know where the ball will come out and for an instant they have no overview of the situation.
- A chain reaction as players pressure the ball.
- If one of the players is free, he can position himself behind the players who are challenging for the ball in the hope of winning the "second" ball.
- If the opposing team has a player who is strong in the air, one player can position himself in front and another can position himself behind.
- It is almost impossible to win a heading duel against some players (e.g. the Czech Jan Koller). It may be better to close down the space around a player who is strong in the air.

Forward pass behind the defenders

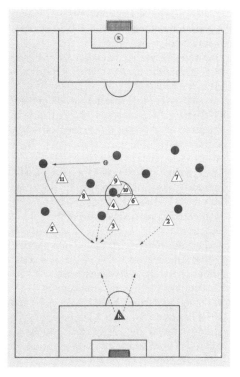

Goalkeeper

The goalkeeper should position himself in the arc on the edge of the penalty area. The chance that an opposing player will score from 60 yards away is virtually negligible. He should be ready to sprint forward to clear the ball if it is played forward over his defenders.

Cooperation between the other defenders

The 3 defenders should not position themselves too far apart. The defenders should aim to position themselves between the ball and an opponent. The two full backs must cover the central defender's back.

If we aim to pressure the opposition as far up the field as possible, there will inevitably be more space between our defenders and our goal. Good positional play by the central defender, good cooperation in the defensive line and good positional play by the goalkeeper can prevent the opposition from creating scoring chances.

Central defender (3)

The central defender must be able to read the opposing team's build-up play. If the opposing team plays a long ball forward, the defender must leave his direct opponent and cover the zone. This gives him a lead over his opponent, which can make it easier for him to deal with the forward ball.

Pressing in youth soccer

The principles that apply to young soccer players are not the same as those that apply to mature players. Adult soccer is all about the final result. The zone that the team occupies when it exerts pressure on the opposition is chosen purely with the aim of winning. Youth soccer, however, is mainly about developing young players.

In top soccer, pressuring the opposition in its own half has been a subject of debate in recent years. The presence of too many players in the limited space in front of the goal has encouraged teams to occupy the zone around the center circle (medium pressing zone).

We have to ask ourselves whether we want to promote this development in youth soccer. In terms of their development, young players can benefit more from pressing in the opposing team's half, where space is limited and there is a high level of resistance. Only in the final phase of the young players' development should the position of the defensive block be made dependent on factors such as the level of skill of the two teams and the final result. Simply copying defensive aspects of adult soccer is not always an ideal solution for the under-14 age group. We therefore take an age-group-specific approach to the subject of pressuring the opposition's build-up play.

10 to12-year-olds
Pressing is not a key topic for 10 to 12-year-olds. They quickly pick up insights about play when in possession of the ball, and learning how to play 11v11 should take up most of the training sessions. However, the coach can motivate the players to exert pressure on the opposition. This takes the players closer to the opposition's goal, which is good for the attacking effectiveness of players with a limited action radius.

12 to 14-year-olds
The players in this age group have acquired more insight. They are more aware of how to play when in possession and how to play to play when the opposition has possession. The players should be able to take part in all the main phases of the game. They are mature enough to handle different game situations. From the age of 14 they are ready for pressing play. Depending on the time available and the players' level of skill, a complete session can be devoted to this, or just a drill or part of a drill.

14 to 16-year-olds
From this age, players must learn about every opportunity of making life difficult for the opposition. Pressuring the opposition is a key aspect of this. They must be able to decide where to exert pressure. The philosophy is that "pressing is a means of gaining possession, and should not be carried out just for its own sake." If there is sufficient coaching time available, pressing can be dealt with progressively over a series of training sessions.

17 and 18-year-olds
The players must carry out their tasks exactly, rather than interpreting them as they see fit, when the opposition has possession. The coach defines the tactics and assigns specific tasks and functions to the players. The zone where the opposition is put under pressure is chosen purely for the purpose of winning the game. Pressing is dealt with progressively.

Coaching how to defend

Three or four defenders?

In modern soccer, teams often have a four-man defense. In my view, defending plays an important part in the development of young soccer players. Players who cannot pressure their opponents effectively, or have problems in 1v1 situations, or fail to master the essentials of positional play when the opposing team has the ball face a difficult future. Targeted development in this key part of the game is essential.

Coaches must take an age-appropriate approach to influencing young players with regard to the situation "opposition in possession." Too many coaches copy the four-man defense adopted by their colleagues in adult soccer and this is not good for the development of young soccer players.

In recent years a lot of attention has been paid to the four-man defense and playing zonally. This approach has gradually spread to youth soccer. In view of the differences between youth soccer and adult soccer, we need to take a closer look at this.

In youth soccer, the fourth defender should play as far forward as possible. In adult soccer he is an additional "lock" on the door and will often have to play a covering role.

Adult soccer

Adult soccer is about getting a result. The team's organization when the opposing team has the ball serves as a basis for this. The players' roles on the field correlate with their skills; a defender who is slow on the turn will not be asked to mark one on one. A player's weak points are often camouflaged by other players, or he is positioned where his skills can be optimally utilized.

Youth soccer

Youth soccer is about the development of young soccer players. Winning games is important but it must not be at the cost of the development philosophy. A player who is unable to turn quickly must be confronted with his shortcomings. He must go through a development process in which he learns to play one against one.

Defense in adult soccer
– 4 zonal defenders

In adult soccer, the aims are to avoid giving away scoring chances and to prevent the opposition from scoring goals.

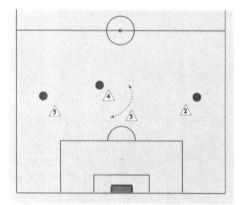

In practice, the four defenders should take up position close to each other. In reality, however, things may look very different. One of the central defenders often provides cover for the other central defender. Above all, the defenders try to remain organized and take as few positional risks as possible. The players cover each other's mistakes and have one aim, i.e. to avoid conceding a goal. Although in theory a lot is said about "zonal defense" and "covering each other in a line," one of the central defenders is virtually a sweeper. The players have a purely defensive role and have little impact on the play when the team has possession. This way of playing is effective in terms of getting a result, but gives the players few development opportunities.

Defense in youth soccer
– 3 defenders and a defensive midfielder

The aims of young soccer players are the same as those of adult players. They want to avoid giving away scoring chances and conceding goals. However, these aims are also a means to promote the development of the players. The way in which the team plays is oriented toward the individual development process of the players.

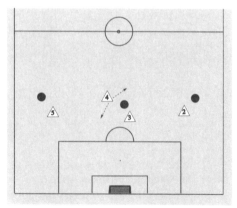

In this way of playing, the fourth defensive player (no. 4) is a defensive midfielder. Depending on the situation he will mainly play in front of or alongside the central defender (3), and in some cases he may provide cover behind the central defender. This way of playing demands a lot of concentration from the defenders, and a good understanding of how to cooperate. All the players have maximum responsibility with regard to their position.

When the team has possession, the defensive midfielder (4) plays in front of the defense. The central defender (3) and the defensive midfielder (4) may sometimes swap positions. This also influences the soccer ability of the players.

The role of the defensive midfielder

Depending on the situation, the defensive
midfielder may play in front of, in line with or
behind the defensive line.

Behind the defensive line
When the opposing team's attacking midfielder infiltrates the defense.

In the defensive line
The opposing team's attacking midfielder
plays in an advanced position.

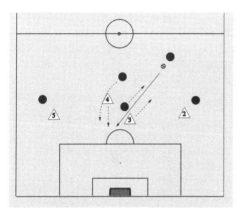 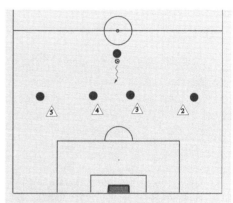

The opposing team's attacking midfielder (10)
makes a forward run. The defensive midfielder
(4) picks him up and covers the space behind
the central defender (3).

In this case the defensive midfielder (4)
must position himself alongside the central
defender (3).

In front of the defensive line
Shielding the defensive line

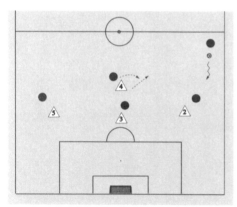

In this situation the defensive midfielder (4) plays in front of the defensive line. As well as covering the opposing team's attacking midfielder (10), he is also responsible for shielding the passing line to the opposing team's striker (9).

Advantages and disadvantages of 3 and 4 defenders

3 defenders

Advantages
- Greater demands with regard to 1v1 challenges and defensive positional play
- More demands on the individual players when the team has possession
- The players have to act faster

Disadvantages
- There is more space on the flanks
- Fewer variations (defenders pushing up) are possible

4 defenders

Advantages
Opposing team in possession
- With 4 defenders in the last line, there is more security when the opposing team has the ball.

Own team in possession
- More variations are possible. One of the players can push forward when the team has possession.

Disadvantages
Opposing team in possession
- When the opposing team has possession, fewer demands are made on the individual players. The weak points of one defender can be compensated for by another.
- In some cases there is too much emphasis on how to play when the opposing team has possession. The 4 defenders stay in position too often.

Own team in possession
- There is less pressure and the players do not have to act as quickly. The central defenders often have more time and space when the team has possession.

Organization when the opposing team has possession (by age group)

10 to 12-year-olds

In the youngest age group, 1-3-4-3 is the preferred system. At this age the focus is mainly on play when in possession. This system guarantees a wide spectrum of developments for all players during this phase. In the defensive line we opt for a 1v1 approach when the opposing team is in possession. This helps the players to learn the individual defensive skills. The defensive demands are high. There is no additional player who can correct mistakes.

12 to 14-year-olds

Defensive skills can be developed still further, and more attention can be paid to cooperation between the players. At this age the role of the defensive midfielder can be gradually explained.

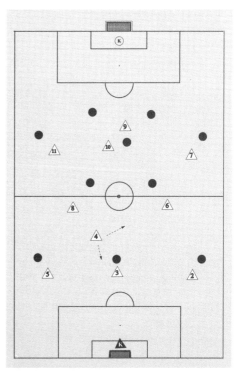

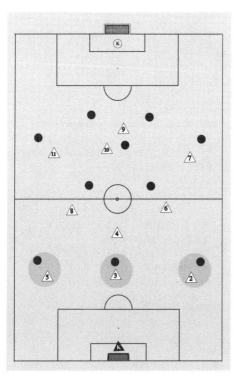

"My experience as a coach teaches me that the best zonal defenders are those who have learned all about man on man marking. In the 1980s, when I still played, the emphasis was on man on man marking. During the 1990s we moved toward zonal defense. Now young players learn only the philosophy of zonal defense. This cannot be right. Ultimately it is always the individual skills of the defender – ability to anticipate, strength in the tackle, etc. – that determine whether he can win the ball or not!"

Emilio Ferrara

14 to 18-year-olds

In this age group, too, the individual development of the players continues. The way in which games are played is directly related to adult soccer. The organization of the team when the opposing team has possession is aligned more to winning the game. The defensive midfielder plays an important role here. How the defensive midfielder plays depends on the strength of the opposing team and the score. The carefree approach of the 12 to 14-year-olds makes way for more realism.

"The 10 to 12-year-olds of FC Ghent play one on one in defense. Jack is a solid defender, but a bit slow. The coach thinks that the team will concede a lot of goals if it plays one on one in defense with Jack as a central defender, so he decides to play a line of 4 defenders with a sweeper behind them."

If we look at the team's aims when the opposing team has possession (regain possession as quickly as possible – prevent the opposing team from scoring), introducing an additional defender will probably bring the greatest short-term gain. In our example, however, this approach has too little impact on Jack's development. It might help the team to achieve its aims, but only at the cost of the individual player's development. Jack's weak points are covered up.

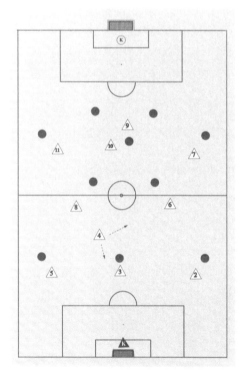

10 to 12-year-olds
3 defenders
Individual development
- Learning about 1 on 1 and defensive skills.

12 to 14-year-olds
3 defenders with or without a defensive midfielder
Individual and collective development
- Learning about 1 on 1 and defensive skills.
- Learning to cooperate with each other

14 to 18-year-olds
3 defenders with defensive midfielder
Collective development
- Optimization of cooperation with each other with regard to the strengths and weaknesses of teammates and opposing players

THE SHAPE OF THE TEAM WHEN THE OPPOSITION HAS POSSESSION

When the opposition has possession, the team can adopt various formations.

Some tips:
- The result is subordinate to the players' development
- Don't change the formation too often. Ensure that space is created in front of the opposition's goal.
- Choose a formation that helps the players' development.
- Ensure that the players all have to go forward.
- Use your own philosophy as the basis.
- Remain true to your philosophy, even if the opposing team is very strong.
- Explain to the players why you have chosen the given formation.
- Ensure that the players are confronted with the all the obstacles of the game.

1-3-4-3 v 1-4-3-3 triangle with apex pointing forward

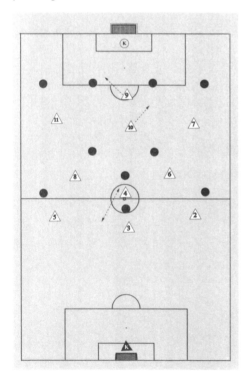

1-3-4-3 v 1-4-3-3 triangle, with apex pointing backward

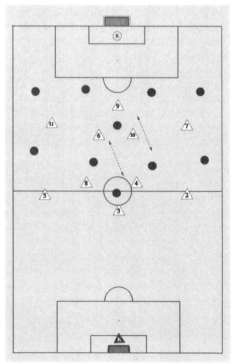

- The right and left backs (2 and 5) and the central defender (3) play in a 3-man defensive line.
- The right and left midfielders (6 and 8) mark the controlling midfielders.
- The defensive midfielder (4) marks the attacking midfielder.
- The striker (9) and the withdrawn striker (10) mark the two central defenders.
- The right and left wingers (7 and 11) mark the full backs.

- The right and left backs (2 and 5) and the central defender (3) play in a 3-man defensive line.
- The defensive midfielder (4) and the left midfielder (8) mark the two attacking midfielders.
- The right midfielder (6) pushes forward.
- The right midfielder and the withdrawn striker (10) both mark the opposition's controlling midfielder.

Depending on the strength of the opposing team:
- The withdrawn striker may or may or may not push forward to be level with the striker
- The defensive midfielder and the right and left midfielders can position themselves in a line.

1-3-4-3 v 1-4-4-2 with a central diamond   **1-3-4-3 v 1-4-4-2**

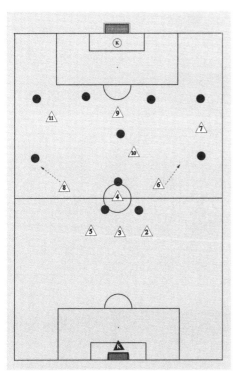
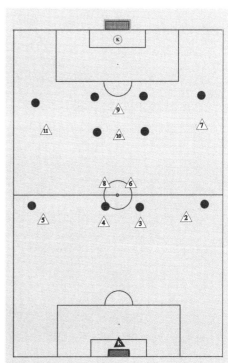

- The right and left backs (2 and 5) and the central defender (3) play in a 3-man defensive line.
- The right and left midfielders (6 and 8) mark the wingers.
- The defensive midfielder (4) marks the attacking midfielder.
- The withdrawn striker (10) marks the defensive midfielder.

- The central defender (3) and the defensive midfielder (4) mark the two strikers.
- The right and left backs (2 and 5) mark the right and left wingers.
- The right and left midfielders (6 and 8) mark the midfielders.

1-3-4-3 v 1-4-4-2 with a central diamond

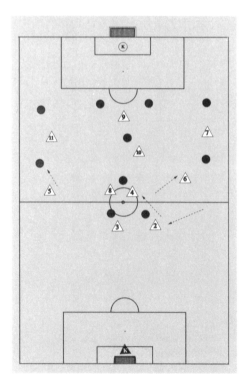

- The right back (2) moves inside and marks one of the two strikers.
- The central defender (3) marks the other striker.
- The defensive midfielder (4) marks the attacking midfielder, and the right midfielder (6) pushes forward and marks the left midfielder.
- The left back (5) marks the right midfielder.

Must young attackers carry out defensive tasks?

"The first line of defense is the attackers." Not every attacker is a born defender. Some attackers (e.g. Romario) have such outstanding offensive skills that they are not required to carry out defensive duties, so their teammates have to perform these for them. Some attackers are poor defenders. It is important, however, for the players to be confronted with the basic tasks on the field. When the opposing team has possession, the attackers must take up positions between the ball and their own goal. This reduces the space available to the opposition. A defender who cannot tackle can increase his team's chances of winning the ball back just by tracking an opponent.

THE PRINCIPLES OF DEFENDING

Position relative to the ball

To put an opponent under pressure, we must deprive him of time and space. When closing down space, there are three standard situations:

- Ball on the left side of the field
- Ball in the center
- Ball on the right side of the field

Ball on the left side of the field

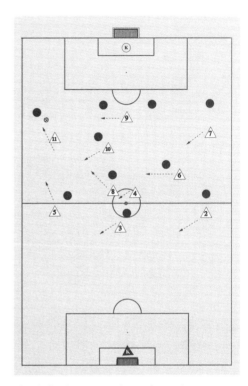

The defending team closes down the space of the left side of the field. The position of the ball is important. The players on the other side of the field move infield and push toward the side where the ball is.

Ball in the center of the field

Ball on the right side of the field

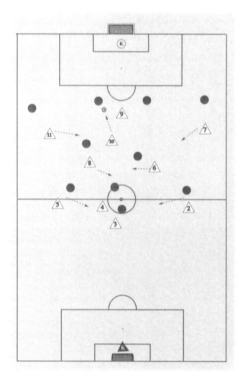

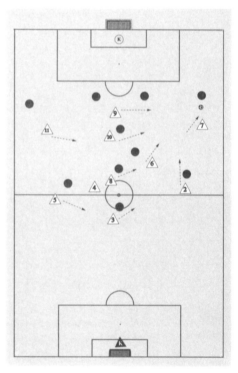

When the ball is in the center, the main defensive aim is to block the shortest path to the goal, i.e. down the middle. The players on the flanks move infield and provide cover for the central players.

When the ball is on the right side of the field, the players on the left move infield. On the right side of the field, the defenders close down the space and mark their opponents closely.

"When the ball is moving, we have to be moving too!"

Wim Koevermans

"The player closest to the ball puts maximum pressure on the player in possession. The other players support him. The last man is always free. He can give the signal to pressure the ball. The player closest to the ball starts. The others must support him intelligently."

Gerrie Mühren
Ex professional soccer player with Ajax Amsterdam, Seville (Spain), etc.

41

Squeezing

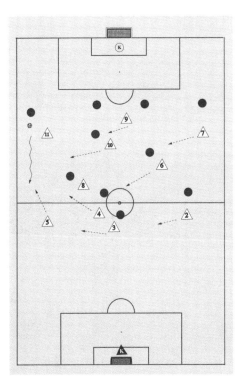

See the man, see the ball

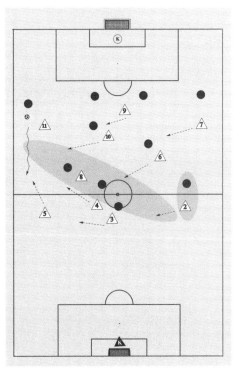

- Move inside toward the ball.
- This means that there is less space on the side where the ball is.
- A defender must not stand level with his opponent, as this leaves space behind the defender's back.
- When the ball is played to his opponent, he must have a genuine chance of intercepting it.
- The extent of the squeeze depends on the distance from the ball and the opponent and the location on the field. When the ball is played in to an opponent, the defender tries to intercept it or to exert pressure as the opponent receives the ball.

- Stand at an angle, so that the ball and your direct opponent are both in your field of view.

The lines must stay close together

Pushing forward

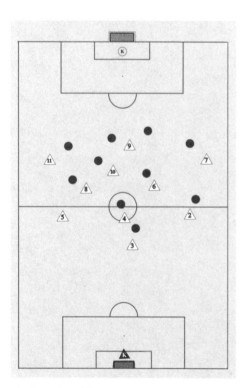

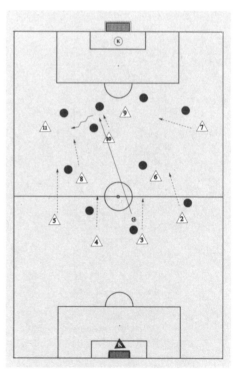

The lines should be 35 to 40 yards apart. If the distance between them is wider, opponents have more chance to escape.

We push forward when:
- an opponent makes a back pass
- when the ball is cleared upfield
- when a counterattack is started

Pushing forward is synonymous with operating the offside trap. Its purpose is to ensure that the lines stay close together. All the lines must move forward the same distance. It is pointless if only the defensive line pushes forward.

The new offside laws have placed pushing forward in a different light. Players have to be more aware when they allow opponents to move into the free space behind their backs.

Winning territory is essential. The opposing team is forced further back into its own half, i.e. further away from the goal at the other end of the field.

Always cover the route down the center

Mark closely

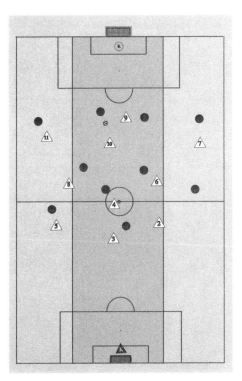

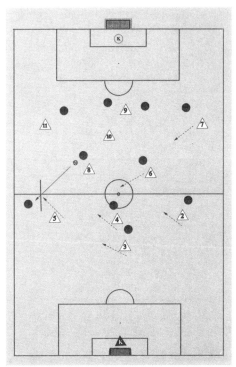

- The defenders stand between the ball and the goal.

- The main aim of marking an opponent closely is to be able to intercept the ball. When the ball is passed to a defender's direct opponent, winning the ball is always the first choice. The defender watches the opposing team's build-up play and tries to anticipate a pass to his direct opponent so he can intercept it (e.g. by getting in front of him).
- If the defender has no chance of winning the ball, he can make life difficult for his opponent by marking him closely and preventing him from making a telling pass.
- The aim is always to react a fraction faster than the direct opponent.

Sufficient defenders

Against 3 attackers

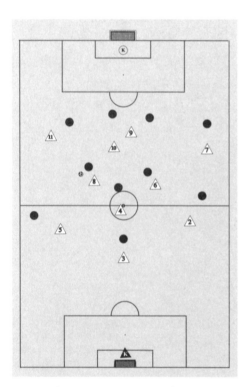

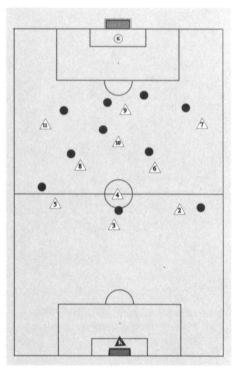

- Depending on the age group of the players and the coaching aims, the coach can opt for a one-on-one situation or a one-man-more situation.
- The number of defenders depends on the number of attackers and the way the opposing team plays. In essence we try to create a one-man-more situation.

- 4 defenders against 3 attackers
- 3 defenders against 2 attackers
- 2 defenders against 1 attacker

The right and left backs (2 and 5) mark the opponent who is in their zone. The central defender (3) marks the opposing team's striker (9). The defensive midfielder (4) switches his role as required. If the central defender needs support, he can drop back to help him.

Against 2 attackers

Against 1 attacker

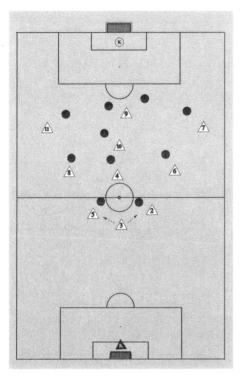

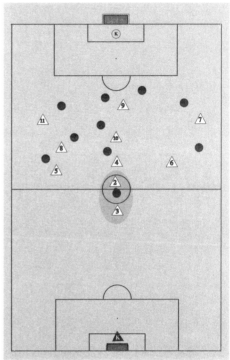

The right and left backs (2 and 5) play zonally, together with the central defender (3). In principle, the central defender can also have a free role, but it is better to play with a three-man zonal defense for the purpose of furthering the development of the defenders. This manner of playing makes high demands on the players.

This situation often arises at restart plays such as corners. It is important that one defender plays in front of the attacker and one player provides cover behind him.

Defending forward

Holding up an opponent

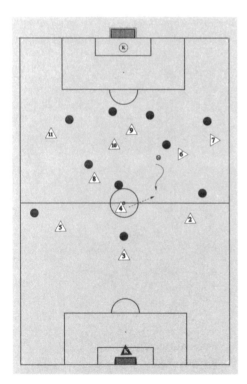

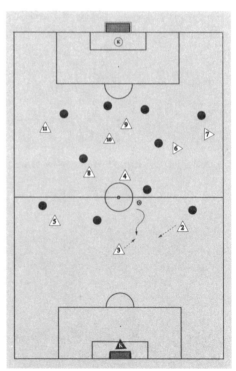

An opposing midfielder has the ball in the center. In this situation the defensive midfielder (4) must go forward to challenge him. The other defenders must also hold their ground rather than dropping back.

Defenders and midfielders often move back toward their own goal, thus creating more space for the player in possession.

Dropping back = Giving away space

In situations where attackers outnumber defenders, it is important for the defenders to hold up the attackers until teammates can get back to help them. This can be done by standing off, slowing down the attacker and forcing him toward the flank. If the goal is in immediate danger, the defender may have to challenge for the ball.

Reducing the space between the goal and the defensive line

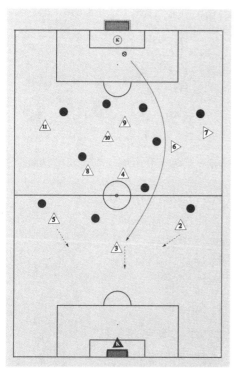

Covering the passing line

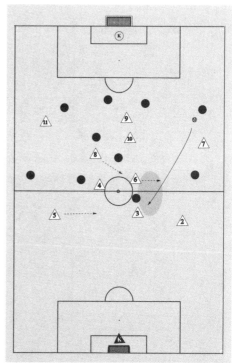

- When the opposing team's goalkeeper kicks the ball out, one or more defenders drop back.
- This means that there is less free space in front of the goal, and the defenders have more time to deal with the ball.

- The left midfielder (8) moves infield and marks an opponent.
- The right midfielder (6) positions himself in front of the defense. This makes it difficult for the opposition to pass to the attacker in the center.
- The defensive midfielder (4) can also cover the passing line.

Defending between two opponents

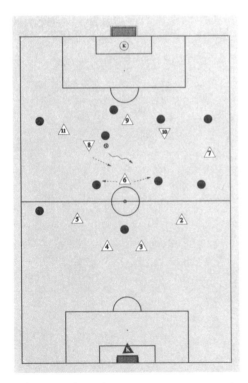 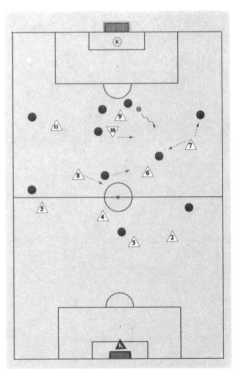

When one player has to cover two opponents
- In this situation the right midfielder (6) can position himself between the two opponents.

When providing support for a teammate
- The right winger (7) positions himself between the left back and the left midfielder of the opposing team.
- The position of the wingers depends on the play of the team in possession.

Don't defend on the center line

Stand on the same level

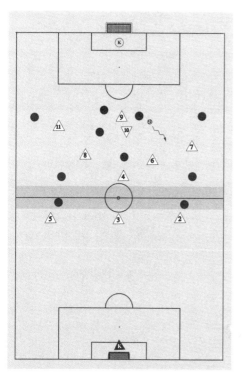

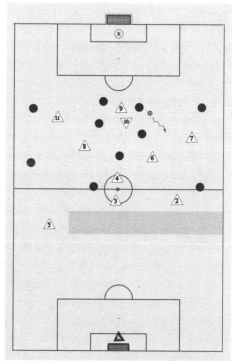

If a team defends on the center line, this gives the opposing attackers an advantage. They can easily infiltrate the defense and avoid being caught by the offside trap. When the opposing team has possession, it is important to defend a few yards before the center line.

If the defense is not on the same level, there is more free space on the side of the field where the ball is. An opponent can easily infiltrate the defense and avoid being caught by the offside trap. It is better for the defenders to stand level with each other.

Following the player with the ball

Examples

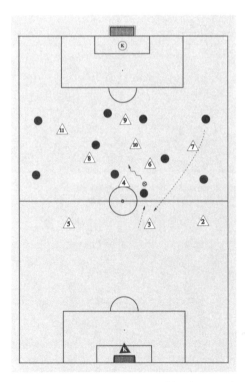

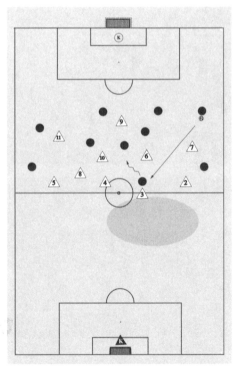

- When an attacker takes the ball back toward his own goal, the defender who is marking him should follow.
- If the central defender would be drawn too far out of position by following the striker, a teammate (e.g. the defensive midfielder) should take over and follow the striker.

The decision on whether or not to follow an opponent depends on the location on the field and whether or not the opponent has the ball. The players' levels of ability also play a role. A player who is superior to his opponent can be put in a 1v1 situation more easily.

If the opponent is in or around the center circle, it is better to let him go. There is no direct danger, and following him may leave space that can be exploited by the opposition.

> "If you get a 50% grade in school, you have succeeded. If you give only 70% in a 1v1 situation, it is insufficient."
>
> *Hein Vanhazebrouck*

Playing zonally

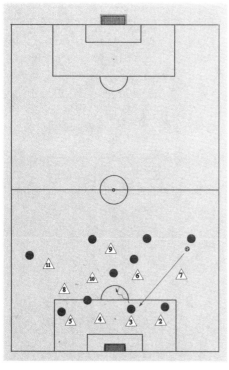

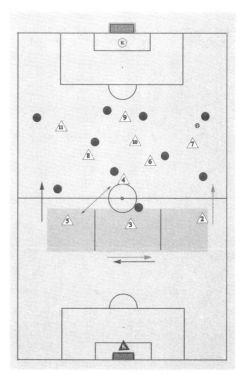

In your own penalty area, it is better to get close to your opponent and stay with him.

Within 20 to 25 yards of the goal, the attacking players must be marked closely.

When the opposing team has possession, you must be aware of

- Your own strengths
- The strengths of your direct opponent
- The strengths of the opposing team
- The strengths of your own team

- In this formation the defensive midfielder (4) plays both in front of and in the defensive line.
- The defensive line is mainly covered by the full backs (2 and 5) and the central defender (3). The defensive midfielder has more of a supporting role.
- The players stay in their zone.
- The players push toward the side of the field where the ball is (see "Squeezing").

Takeovers

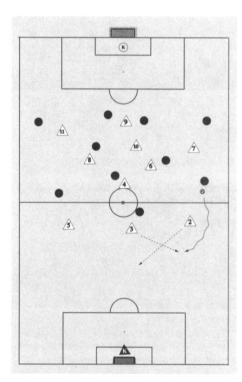

- In some situations players are bypassed and their positions have to be taken over by others.
- In this situation the right back (2) has been left behind by his direct opponent.
- The central defender (3) leaves the center and takes over the right back's position.
- The right back gets back as quickly as he can and takes over the central defender's position.

As a defender, if your opponent takes the ball past you, you have to get back toward your own goal as quickly as possible.

1v1 SITUATIONS

1v1 situations play a leading role in coaching for the "opposition in possession" phase. Besides the collective task (How can we win the ball?), the individual encouragement of 1v1 situations plays an important role in the development of defenders. The most important 1v1 situations are:

1v1 with opponent in front
1v1 with opponent alongside
1v1 with opponent behind

Left footed, right footed – indicate the opponent's strongest foot to your teammate.

A) 1v1 with opponent in front

"Don't sell yourself!"

A Premier League defender

Coaching points:
- Pressure your opponent. Come toward the ball and close down the space.
- Stand with your weight on the balls of your feet – you can react faster.
- Stand at an angle to your opponent with your feet apart – you can turn more quickly if your opponent makes a run with the ball.
- Depending on the situation, try to channel your opponent to the outside, to the inside, or onto his weaker foot.
- Knees bent, keep low.
- Don't dive in for the ball.
- Stay cool and alert. A player who remains cool in a 1v1 situation has the best chance of success.
- Fight for the ball, using controlled aggression. You have to want to win the ball.
- Stay on your feet. A tackle is a last resort.
- Analyze your opponent. Is he the type of player who tries to take the ball past a defender by reacting to his movements, or is he a skillful dribbler?

B) 1v1: marking an opponent

Coaching points:
- Stand at an angle so that you can turn faster.
- Let your opponent feel that you are there. Challenge aggressively but fairly.
- You can't always win a 1v1 confrontation. Try to anticipate the play and get to the ball first.
- Follow your opponent and stay close to him so that he has as little space as possible.

Challenging for the ball
- Choose the right moment to challenge for the ball. If you dive in you may give your opponent the chance to take the ball past you.

- The most suitable moment to challenge for the ball is when the opponent is half turned. The defender has a good view of the ball and the attacker often has all his weight on one foot and is therefore more vulnerable.

Getting in front of an opponent
- If an opponent receives a pass from the side, it is not a good idea to get in front of him. He is often at an angle and can easily use his body to turn away from his marker. Getting in front of an opponent is less risky when a pass is played forward.

A 1v1 confrontation is about winning the ball and not just exerting pressure on an opponent.

C) 1v1 situation with opponent alongside

Before the 1v1:
- The phase before the 1v1 confrontation is important. Reading the situation correctly can give you the advantage.

- Stand at an angle; this can give you a few yards start.

- Try to cut across the line of the ball, between the opposing player and the ball. This slows the opponent's run and makes him cover more ground to reach the ball.

1v1:
- Make yourself as wide as you can.

- Challenge for the ball when your opponent has his weight on the outside foot. This means that he can't take corrective action with his other foot and will lose his balance more easily.
- Try to get your shoulder in front of your opponent's shoulder.
- Use your weight, but don't give away a free kick.
- A tackle is a last resort. Going to ground takes you out of the play.

- A push with the shoulder just as an attacker shoots or makes a forward pass can affect his precision. Choose the moment when your opponent's weight is on one foot.
- If your opponent goes past you, a tap on the sole of his foot may put him off balance so that you can overtake him.

The fastest defender does not always win a 1v1 confrontation. Position relative to the ball and the location on the field are often decisive.

Communication

"Left footer"
The opposing player's left foot is his stronger foot.

"Right footer"
The opposing player's right foot is his stronger foot.

"Go with him"
The opposing player tries to drop off his marker; the marker should follow him.

"Go to him"
An opponent comes forward with the ball and there is space between him and his marker.

"Careful"
Don't give away a free kick.

"Don't dive in"
Don't dive in at your opponent

"Squeeze"
Push toward the side of the field where the ball is.

"Clear it"
Kick the ball upfield.

Defensive headers (after the goalkeeper kicks the ball out)

Coaching points:
- The defender's technique depends on his style and strengths.
  - One-footed take-off
  - Two-footed take-off
  - Jump at an angle to the flight of the ball
  - Jump square on to the path of the ball

- Leave sufficient space between yourself and the attacker. The advantages are:
  - It is easier to take a short run before jumping.
  - It is easier to get in front of the attacker.
  - You can jump higher

- Hold your arms wide as you jump

- When you jump, you can hold your arm above the defender's shoulder. This impedes him slightly as he jumps.

- Land with one foot in front of the other. This means that you can react more quickly to the next phase.

Crosses/corners

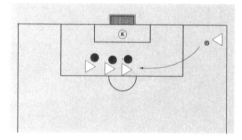

- Stay close to your opponent
- Maintain "contact" (hand, shoulder) with your opponent

- Always try to be just in front of your opponent (5 – 10 inches) to prevent him cutting across in front of you.
- If the ball goes over your head there is still time to take corrective action.
- Stand at an angle so that you can see both the ball and your opponent.

> "Most defenders watch the ball and not their immediate opponent."
>
> *Aimé Antheunis*

COACHING METHOD
Coaching the aims of the game and soccer problems

10 to 14-year olds

COACHING THE AIMS OF THE GAME

Tips:

The players
In this age group there are big differences in height and strength, and smaller players therefore sometimes tend to avoid 1v1 confrontations. Drills designed to accustom the players to 1v1 situations are suitable here. Such drills can involve 100% resistance (opponent in front, opponent alongside, opponent behind).

10 to 12-year-olds: Most 10 to 12-year-olds have enough natural enthusiasm to be able to grasp the principles of defending.

12 to 14-year-olds: The principles of playing when the opposition has possession are not always properly understood. There is sometimes a lack of enthusiasm with regard to this phase of the game.

Young players sometimes tend toward "shadow" defending – they pressure the player in possession, but don't try to win the ball.

Training sessions
The emphasis is on 1v1 situations. Winning confrontations with a direct opponent is the dominant aspect in this module. 1v1 drills, positional drills and small sided games (from 2v1 to 5v5) can be used. Drills with 2 lines (from 6v5 to 8v7) are also suitable. We end with an 8v8 game drill or, sometimes, 11v11.

10 to 12-year-olds: The 10 to 12-year-olds can best start with small drills. All drills from 1v2 to 5v5 are eminently suitable for learning the principles of defending. Special emphasis should be put on 1v1. In the second phase, drills with 2 lines can be introduced. These require more insight from the players.

12 to 14-year-olds: These players have 2 years of experience with 11v11. They have more insight.

The lessons learned in the 10 to 12-year-old group are continued. The coach can introduce drills with more players sooner (2 lines). The principles of collective defense can be introduced.

The focus on pressuring the opposing team in its own half means that there is less emphasis on the possession phase. Some sessions should therefore be mainly devoted to positional drills, in which possession is central,

The coach
The right moment to exert pressure is determined by the players, not the coach. Young players tend to exert pressure continuously, which requires a lot of energy. During the game, analyze the moments when pressing would be advantageous and help the players to conserve their energy.

10 to 12-year-olds: The players can learn how to jointly pressure the player on the ball and win possession as soon as possible. The coach can give tips to individuals (e.g. what to do in 1v1 situations). He can also give simple instructions to the team (e.g. try to work together).

12 to 14-year-olds: A game is made up of a sequence of game moments. The players must now be more aware of this. Not every moment is suitable for exerting pressure on the opposition. The players must gradually think more about the team rather than just themselves. The coach must steadily encourage this.

Pressing is ball-oriented. Marking is player-oriented.

The match

Pressing is about winning the ball rather than causing the opposition to lose the ball. In the initial phase the players tend to forget about possession. There is no transition from the pressing phase to a calm possession phase. As a result, possession is frequently lost. Keeping calm and maintaining a good overview are important in this module.

> *Give positive encouragement to players who neglect to defend.*

10 to 12-year-olds: In view of the limited action radius of the players, it is easier to exert pressure on the ball. Goal kicks in particular can cause problems.

12 to 14-year-olds: In this age group, the obstacles are closer to real match situations. The players have a wider action radius. They are able to play long passes. They must learn to exert pressure more efficiently, as the opposing team can escape the pressure relatively easily.

> *We don't exert pressure for its own sake; we want to win the ball.*

Aim

> The defending module for 10 to 14-year-olds
> Aim: To learn 11v11
> "Learning to cope with match-related obstacles"
> Own position – 2 lines

Drills:

Discovery phase

1v1
- Opponent in front
- Opponent behind
- Opponent alongside

Positional training

1 : 2 =>
2 : 2 =>
2 : 3 =>
3 : 3 =>
3 : 4 =>
4 : 4 =>
4 : 5 =>

Line training, 2 lines

5 : 6 =>
6 : 6 =>
6 : 7 =>
7 : 7 =>
7 : 8 =>

Training phase

Positional training

1 : 2 =>
2 : 2 =>
2 : 3 =>
3 : 3 =>
3 : 4 =>
4 : 4 =>
4 : 5 =>

Line training, 2 lines

5 : 6 =>
6 : 6 =>
6 : 7 =>
7 : 7 =>
7 : 8 =>

Game phase

Match-related drill (8v8 or 11v11)

Practical example:
Learning one of the aims of the game

Young players do not have much insight when they play 11v11. They need to develop further before they can play in a 1-3-4-3 formation. We therefore speak of learning one of the aims of the game in this age group. The players learn the principles of one of the aims of the game. The examples are aimed at young soccer players who have not mastered the basic principles of defending.

Learning one of the aims of the game

We have chosen the following sequence for the players to learn one of the aims of the game.

We determine:

The starting situation
 The age group
 The level
 The number of training sessions per week
 The starting level of the players

The development objective
 What do we want to achieve?

We then choose the following steps:

1. What playing system are we going to choose?
2. Which module do we want to choose?
3. Which players are we looking at?
4. Which part of the field and in which direction?
5. What drills should we choose?
6. How should we factor in the age-typical aspects?
7. How should we draw up the schedule?
8. What should be the content of the training session?

We determine
The starting situation:

Age group: 10 to 12-year-olds
Level: Regional amateur level
Number of training sessions per week: 2
Starting level of the players:
The players are not familiar with the principles of defending in an 11v11 context.

The development objective:
To learn the defensive principles
- Exerting pressure on the ball
- Closing down space (squeezing)
- Winning the ball

1. What playing system are we going to choose?
The players in this age group play in a 1-3-4-3 formation.

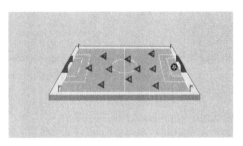

2. Which module do we want to choose?
The defending module.

3. Which players are we looking at?

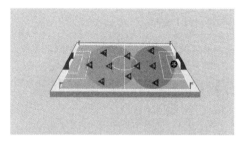

All the players, with the emphasis on the defenders and the goalkeeper.

4. Which part of the field and in which direction?

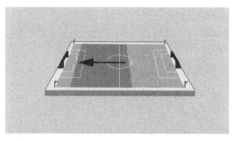

In the opposing team's half, in the direction of the opposing team's goal.

5. What drills should we choose?

- Passing and shooting drills.
- 1v1 drills
- Positional training (from 1v2 to 5v5).
- Line training with 2 lines (from 5v6 to 8v8).

In the 1v1 drills the players learn all the skills needed for defending. Positional training is ideal for learning simple defensive skills. In the line drills, the players learn how the two lines work together (e.g. defenders and goalkeeper with midfielders). In view of the level of the players, we only work with drills up to 5v5.

6. How should we factor in the age-typical aspects?

The 10 to 14 age group is in the learning phase for 11v11. Besides developing general skills, it is important to put the players more or less in their own positions. There is not much point in placing attackers in defensive positions when coaching defensive play. The players have a lot of time necessary just to absorb the developments relating to their own position.

7. How should we draw up the schedule?

This schedule is simply an example. Coaches should not simply copy it. Factors such as enjoyment, form on the day, the translation of the aim of the game in practice and the time of year all influence the scheduling of the training sessions. Coaches must translate the aim of the game into practice in ways that suit their own situation.

8. What should be the content of the training session?

The development objectives of the sessions.

Session 1: The coach starts with various 1v1 drills (defender in front, defender alongside, defender behind). In the training phase the players carry out simple drills (2v3, 3v3). We end the session with a match-related drill (8v8).

Session 2: The coach continues the positional training from the previous session (2v2, 3v3). In the training phase the defenders occupy their own positions and play 4 + goalkeeper v 5. We end with a match-related drill (8v8).

Session 3: We confront the players with the 1v1 drills again in the discovery phase. In the training phase the players are given positional coaching and work on the tips from the discovery phase (1v1). We end the session with a free match-related drill (8v8).

Tuesday	**training**	**tactical**	**flank module**	**session 1**
Thursday	**training**	**tactical**	**defense module**	**session 2**
Saturday	match			
Tuesday	training	technical/changing direction and turning/ positional play/match-related drill		
Thursday	**training**	**tactical**	**defense module**	**session 3**
Saturday	match			
Tuesday	training	Positional play (4v2/5v2/match-related drill)		
Thursday	**training**	**tactical**	**defense module**	**session 4**
Saturday	match			

Session 4: We start with the basic principles of defending. 2v3 and 3v3 drills are again chosen. In the training phase we continue with the 4 + goalkeeper v 5 positional training. Positional tips are given. We end the session with a match-related drill.

Session 1
Development objective of the session
The coach starts with various 1v1 drills (defender in front, defender alongside, defender
behind). In the training phase the players carry
out simple drills (2v3, 3v3). We end the session
with a match-related drill (8v8).

Discovery phase: 1v1 drills
Training phase: Positional training
                    (2v3,3v3)
Game phase: Match-related drill (8v8,
                    depending on the number
                    of available players)

Content of the session
Discovery phase:
1v1 drills

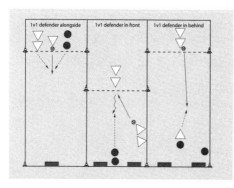

Organization:
A) Opponent alongside
- The ball is played to the attacker and
  defender – 1v1.
- The attacker can score in the small goal.
- The defender can score by playing the ball to
  a teammate on the imaginary line.

B) Opponent in front
- The ball is played to the attacker – 1v1.
- The attacker can score in the small goal.
- The defender can score by crossing the
  imaginary line with the ball.

C) Opponent behind
- The ball is played to the attacker – 1v1.
- The attacker can lay the ball of to his
  teammate
- The attacker can score in the small goal.
- The defender can score by crossing the
  imaginary line with the ball.

Coaching points:
See "The aims of the game" – 1v1.

Training phase:
positional training (2v3, 3v3)

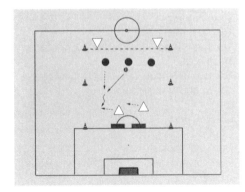

Organization:
- First 2v3, then 3v3.
- The three attackers can score in one of the small goals.
- The two defenders can score by playing the ball to one of their teammates.

Coaching points:
- Exert pressure on the ball.
- Don't sell yourself.
- Push toward the side of the field where the ball is.
- Help each other.

Success moment:
If the defenders score 5 times we choose different defenders.

Game phase:
8v8 (depending on the number of available players)
Free play

Session 2
Development objective of the session
The coach continues the positional training from the previous session (2v2, 3v3). In the training phase the defenders occupy their own positions and play 4 + goalkeeper v 5. We end with a match-related drill (8v8).

Discovery phase: Positional training
                    (2v3, 3v3)
Training phase: Positional training
                    (4+GK v 5)
Game phase: Match-related drill (8v8,
                    depending on the number
                    of available players)

Content of the session
Discovery phase:
positional training (2v3, 3v3)

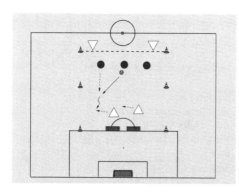

Organization:
- First 2v3, then 3v3.
- The three attackers can score in one of the small goals.
- The two defenders can score by playing the ball to one of their teammates.

Coaching points:
- Exert pressure on the ball.
- Don't sell yourself.
- Push toward the side of the field where the ball is.
- Help each other.

Success moment:
If the defenders score 5 times we choose different defenders.

Training phase:
positional training (4+GK v 5)

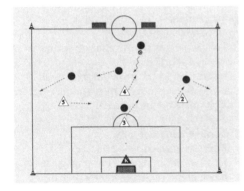

Organization:
- The five attackers can score in the large goal.
- The four defenders can score in one of the small goals.

Coaching points:
- Push toward the side of the field where the ball is.
- Watch your opponent and the ball.
- Don't sell yourself.
- Help each other.

Success moment:
2 x 15 min. Who wins?

Game phase:
8v8 (depending on the number of available players)

Success moment:
1-0 for the defenders. The attackers have 10 minutes to score.

Session 3
Development objective of the session
We confront the players with the 1v1 drills
again in the discovery phase. In the training
phase the players are given positional coaching and work on the tips from the discovery
phase (1v1). We end the session with a free
match-related drill (8v8).

Discovery phase: 1v1 drills
Training phase: Positional training
                    (4+GK v 5)
Game phase: Match-related drill (8v8,
                    depending on the number
                    of available players)

Content of the session
Discovery phase:
1v1 drills

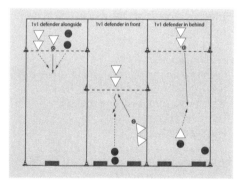

Organization:
A) Opponent alongside
- The ball is played to the attacker and
  defender – 1v1.
- The attacker can score in the small goal.
- The defender can score by playing the ball to
  a teammate on the imaginary line.

B) Opponent in front
- The ball is played to the attacker – 1v1.
- The attacker can score in the small goal.
- The defender can score by crossing the
  imaginary line with the ball.

C) Opponent behind
- The ball is played to the attacker – 1v1.
- The attacker can lay the ball of to his
  teammate
- The attacker can score in the small goal.
- The defender can score by crossing the
  imaginary line with the ball.

Coaching points:
See "The aims of the game" – 1v1.

Training phase:
positional training (4+GK v 5)

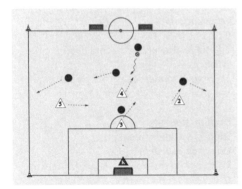

Organization:
- The five attackers can score in the large goal.
- The four defenders can score in one of the small goals.

Coaching points:
- Push toward the side of the field where the ball is.
- Watch your opponent and the ball.
- Don't sell yourself.
- Help each other.

Success moment:
2 x 15 min. Who wins?

Game phase:
8v8 (depending on the number of available players)
Free play

Session 4
Development objective of the session
We start with the basic principles of defending. 2v3 and 3v3 drills are again chosen. In the training phase we continue with the 4 + goalkeeper v 5 positional training. Positional tips are given. We end the session with a match-related drill.

Discovery phase: Positional training
                          (2v3, 3v3)
Training phase: Positional training
                          (4+GK v 5)
Game phase: Match-related drill (8v8,
                          depending on the number
                          of available players)

Content of the session
Discovery phase:
positional training (2v3, 3v3)

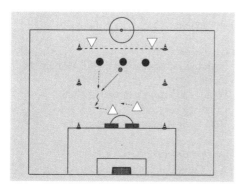

Organization:
- First 2v3, then 3v3.
- The three attackers can score in one of the small goals.
- The two defenders can score by playing the ball to one of their teammates.

Coaching points:
- Exert pressure on the ball.
- Don't sell yourself.
- Push toward the side of the field where the ball is.
- Help each other.

Success moment:
If the defenders score 5 times we choose different defenders.

Training phase:
positional training (4+GK v 5)

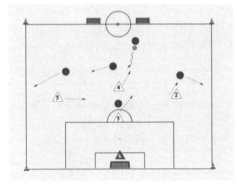

Organization:
- The five attackers can score in the large goal.
- The four defenders can score in one of the small goals.

Coaching points:
- Push toward the side of the field where the ball is.
- Watch your opponent and the ball.
- Don't sell yourself.
- Help each other.

Success moment:
2 x 15 min. Who wins?

Game phase:
8v8 (depending on the number of available players)

Success moment:
1-0 for the defenders. The attackers have 10 minutes to score.

Evaluation

Coaching the aims of the game

- **Do the players enjoy themselves?**
  There is sufficient variation in the drills
  (1v1 drills, match-related drills).

- **Is the development objective achieved?**
  The players have grasped the basic
  principles of defending:
  - Pressing
  - Closing down space (squeezing)
  - Winning the ball

- **Is the number of practice drills in the
  training sessions limited?**
  There are a maximum of 3 drills in each
  training session.

- **Is the number of practice drills in the
  module limited?**
  A total of 4 drills are integrated in the
  module.

- **Is there a good balance between match-
  related and non-match-related drills?**
  The drills all involve a real opponent.

- **Is there a progressive buildup over a
  certain period?**
  Four training sessions are completed over
  a period of 3 weeks. The level of resistance is
  slowly increased.

- **Are there sufficient repetitions for the
  players?**
  All players are sufficiently involved in each
  drill.

- **Is sufficient consideration given to the
  age group of the players?**
  The drills used in these practical examples
  are oriented to the players' age group. The
  content is adjusted to the age of the players.

- **Are the drills adjusted to their level?**
  The drills are applicable at every regional
  level. If they are too difficult, the coach can
  easily adjust them.

- **Do the players have sufficient freedom of
  movement?**
  Sufficient free moments are incorporated.

14 to 18-year olds

PROBLEM ORIENTED COACHING

Tips

The players:

Pressing in the opposition's half depends on an exact analysis of the opposing players. Players in this age group are able to do this independently. Is the direct opponent a right or left-footer? Who is the weakest defender? The analysis enables the team to decide the best way to exert pressure.

14 to 16-year-olds: The results of pressing are not always optimal at this age. The players are sometime too enthusiastic and waste a lot of energy chasing opponents unnecessarily.

17 and 18-year-olds: Pressing is more organized and disciplined. The players are able to read the game well and can collectively choose the right moment to exert pressure on an opponent.

Training sessions:

In the initial phase it may be better to work in small groups so that the players can be influenced individually. Positional drills are the most efficient way to start. Small drills from 1v2 to 4v5 offer lots of options for individual development. Later, in the discovery phase, you can switch directly to drills with 2 lines. In the training phase, depending on the development process, you can introduce drills with 2 and 3 lines. In the final phase you can introduce 8v8 or 11v11, depending on the number of available players. 11v11 is the most suitable after drills with 3 lines.

14 to 16 year olds: The players are able to train collectively with good focus. Individual shortcomings can be dealt with in smaller drills (from 1v2 to 5v5). Coaching of 1v1 situations can be taken further.

17 and 18 year-olds: At this age every game is an aim in itself. Coaching has to be adjusted to this. The players must be able to adapt the way which they exert pressure to the strengths of the opposing players. Larger drills with 2 or 3 lines are ideal for this.

The coach:

In this module the analysis of the opposition's strengths and weaknesses can be very detailed. The focus should not just be on winning the ball but also on what to do after winning it. After all, we exert pressure in order to win possession and create goal-scoring chances.

15 and 16-year-olds: The players must be aware that they have to work hard to win possession of the ball. They sometimes have to make sacrifices to help a teammate, and sometimes their efforts will seem pointless. The coach must convince his players that winning is not self-evident.

17 and 18-year-olds: Each game has to be won. This is our starting point. The mental pressures on the players are greater. Pressing and defending are part of the match preparation and each player has to contribute. The coach gives clear guidelines to his players. If the coach is not happy with how the game is going, he can make changes.

The match:

The match looks like a game between mature players. The opposing team is fully equipped to deal with pressing. Pressing is physically demanding and cannot always be maintained for the full 90 minutes. Players in the older age group are sometimes too enthusiastic and don't wait for the most efficient moment to chase the opposing players. Pressing often has the best results early in the match. Its effectiveness is influenced by factors such as the strength of the opposition, the score, etc. It is therefore not always possible to defend in the opposition's half.

15 and 16-year-olds: The players have to cope with difficult soccer problems. They are often confronted with 1v1 challenges and situations where they have very little space.

17 and 18-year-olds: The play is more mature. The players no longer race after each ball. They wait for the best moment to pressure the opposing players.

Aim

> **The flank module between 14 and 18**
>
> Aim:
> - To perfect playing 11v11
> - To learn how to deal with the manner in which the opposition plays
> - Collective development with regard to
>   - the strengths and weaknesses of the players' own team and the opposition
>   - the players' own positions, the line, the total team

Drills for the discovery phase

1v1 drills - Opponent in front - Opponent behind - Opponent alongside	Positional training 1:2 => 2:2 => 2:3 => 3:3 => 3:4 => 4:5 =>	Line training 2 lines 5:6 => 6:6 => 6:7 => 7:7 => 7:8 =>	Line training 3 lines 7:9 => 8:9 => 9:9 => 9:10 => 10:10 => 10:11 =>

Training phase

Line training 2 lines 5:6 => 6:6 => 6:7 => 7:7 => 7:8 =>	Line training 3 lines 7:9 => 8:9 => 9:9 => 9:10 => 10:11 =>

Game phase

> Match-related drills (8v8 to 11 v11, depending on number of available players)

Practical example
Problem-oriented coaching

As the players get older, we talk of "problem-oriented coaching". The players have played 11v11 for a number of years and have built up a basic knowledge of the manner of playing. The coach can therefore base his coaching more on real match situations. The players know the basic principles of defensive play. If the players in this age group are not sufficiently advanced, the coach can focus on coaching the aims of the game (see example for 10 to 14 year-olds).

Problem-oriented coaching

Problem-oriented coaching involves the following steps.

First we determine:
- The starting situation
- The age group
- The level
- The number of training sessions per week
- The starting level of the players
- The soccer problem – who, what, where, when?
- The development objective – what do we want to achieve?

We then choose the following steps:
1. What playing system are we going to choose?
2. Which module do we want to choose?
3. Which players are we looking at?
4. Which part of the field and in which direction?
5. What drills should we choose?
6. How should we factor in the age-typical aspects?
7. How should we draw up the schedule?
8. What should be the content of the training session?

We determine
The starting situation:

Age group: 16 year olds
Level: Highest youth level
Number of training sessions per week: 4
Starting level of the players: The players are familiar with the aims of defending/pressing.

Soccer problem
When the players press the opposing team, they leave too many escape options. The co-operation between attackers and midfielders is poor. The players don't chase as a unit.

The development objective
Pressing the opposing team in its own half.

1. What playing system are we going to choose?
The players are familiar with a 1-3-4-3 formation.

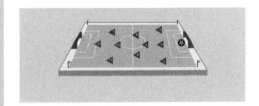

2. Which module do we want to choose?
The defensive play module.

3. Which players are we looking at?
Mainly the attackers, in cooperation with the midfielders.

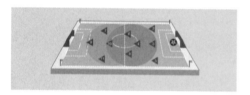

4. Which part of the field and in which direction?
In the opposition's half in the direction of the fixed goal.

5. What drills should we choose?
The following drills can be used for the 14 to 18-year-old age group:
- 1v1 drills.
- Positional training (from 1v2 to 5v5).
- Line training with 2 lines (from 5v6 to 8v8).
- Line training with 3 lines (from 7v8 to 11v11).

Match-related drills are used to coach this soccer problem.

6. How should we factor in the age-typical aspects?
In the oldest age group, the emphasis is on specialization in the player's own position. The position that a player occupies during training sessions corresponds as far as possible to his strongest position.

7. How should we draw up the schedule?
The coach can put his own interpretation on this schedule.

8. What should be the content of the training session?
We have devised 4 fictional training sessions.

Sunday	*match*	During the match the coach is confronted with the following soccer problem. When the players press the opposing team, they leave too many escape options. The cooperation between attackers and midfielders is poor. The players don't chase as a unit.
Monday	training	recuperation training
Tuesday	**training**	**tactical defense module session 1**
Wednesday	training	Passing and shooting drill – positional play – match-related drill
Thursday	**training**	**tactical defense module session 2**
Monday	training	recuperation training
Tuesday	**training**	**tactical defense module session 3**
Wednesday	training	Finishing drill - match-related drill
Thursday	training	11v11 against another team
Sunday	match	The players mark closely on the flank where the ball is. The players on the other flank don't squeeze very effectively toward the flank where the ball is.
Monday	training	recuperation training
Tuesday	training	Finishing drill - match-related drill
Wednesday	training	Passing and shooting drill – positional play – match-related drill
Thursday	**training**	**tactical defense module session 4**
Sunday	match	The players press efficiently again

The development objectives of the training sessions.

Session 1: We start with a positional drill (4v5+goalkeeper). The coaching is focused on the attackers' running lines. In the training phase we expand the drill by introducing midfielders (6v7+goalkeeper). We end with a match drill (8v8).

Session 2: We continue training with 2 lines. We expand from 6v7+goalkeeper to 7v7+goalkeeper. We then translate the principles we have learned into a game of 11v11 (against an older team).

Session 3: In real matches, the coach sees that the midfield and attacking lines are too far apart. We start with 1v1 drills, with the accent on individual skills and defending. We then tackle the problem identified by the coach, using a drill with 2 lines, in which the midfielders have to push forward in support (6v7+goalkeeper). We close with a match-related drill (8v8).

Session 4: The match analysis shows that the players on the other flank do not squeeze toward the flank where the ball is often enough. We start in the discovery phase again with 1v1 with the players in their actual positions. We then switch to the same drill with 3 lines from the previous session. The drill is adapted to the soccer problem. We finish the session with a match-related drill (11v11) against another age group.

In the next real match we see that the players press efficiently again.

Session 1
Development objective of the session
Session 1: We start with a positional drill (4v5+goalkeeper). The coaching is focused on the attackers' running lines. In the training phase we expand the drill by introducing midfielders (6v7+goalkeeper). We end with a match drill (8v8).

Discovery phase: Positional training
(4v5+GK)

Training phase: Line training with 2 lines
(6v7+GK)

Game phase: Match-related drill (8v8, depending on the number of available players)

Content of the session
Discovery phase:
positional training (4v5+GK)

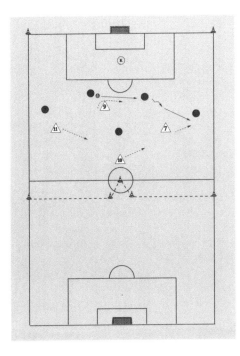

Organization:
- The 5 defenders can score by running with ball across one of the two imaginary lines of the triangle.
- The 4 attackers can score in the large goal.

Coaching points:
Striker (9)
- Force the central defender toward the flank.
- Try to prevent the opposing team from playing the ball past you.

Withdrawn striker (10)
Pick up the defensive midfielder.

Winger (7)
Force your opponent toward the flank

Winger (11)
Squeeze toward the flank where the ball is.

**Training phase:
positional training (6v7+GK)**

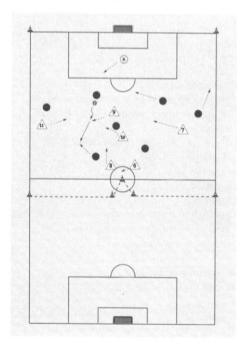

Organization:
- The 7 defenders can score by running with ball across one of the two imaginary lines of the triangle.
- The 6 attackers and midfielders can score in the large goal.

Coaching points:
Striker (9)
- Force the central defender toward the flank.
- Try to prevent the opposing team from playing the ball past you.

Withdrawn striker (10)
Pick up the defensive midfielder.

Winger (7)
Force your opponent toward the flank

Winger (11)
Squeeze toward the flank where the ball is.

Midfielders (6 and 8)
Pick up your direct opponent. Cover each other.

Success moment:
A goal scored after one of the defenders loses the ball counts double.

Game phase:
8v8 (depending on the number of available players)

Success moment:
A goal scored after winning the ball in the opposition's half counts double.

Session 2
Development objective of the session
Session 2: We continue training with 2 lines. We expand from 6v7+goalkeeper to 7v7+goalkeeper. We then translate the principles we have learned into a game of 11v11 (against an older team).

Discovery phase: Line training with 2 lines
                   (6v7+GK - 7v7+GK)
Game phase: Match-related drill (11v11,
                   depending on the number
                   of available players)

Content of the session
Discovery phase:
6v7+GK - 7v7+GK

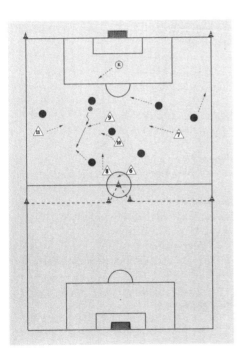

Organization:
- The 7 defenders can score by crossing one of the two imaginary lines of the triangle with the ball.
- The 6 attackers and midfielders can score in the large goal.

Coaching points:
Striker (9)
- Force the central defender toward the flank.
- Try to prevent the opposing team from playing the ball past you.

Withdrawn striker (10)
Pick up the defensive midfielder.

Winger (7)
Force your opponent toward the flank

Winger (11)
Squeeze toward the flank where the ball is.

Midfielders (6 and 8)
Pick up your direct opponent. Cover each other.

Success moment:
A goal scored after one of the defenders loses the ball counts double.

Game phase: 11v11 (against an older team)

Session 3
Development objective of the session
Session 3: In real matches, the coach sees that the midfield and attacking lines are too far apart. We start with 1v1 drills, with the accent on individual skills and defending. We then tackle the problem identified by the coach, using a drill with 2 lines, in which the midfielders have to push forward in support (6v7+goalkeeper). We close with a match-related drill (8v8).

Discovery phase:	1v1 with players in their own positions
Training phase:	Line training with 3 lines (6v7+GK)
Game phase:	Match-related drill (8v8, depending on the number of available players)

Content of the session
Discovery phase:
1v1 with players in their own positions

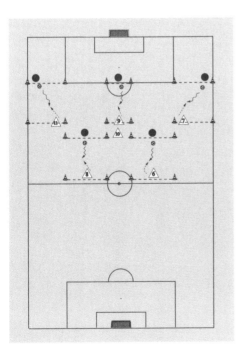

Organization:
Each player stands in a zone that corresponds to his match position.
- 1v1 with opponent
- Ensure that the players have sufficient pauses

Coaching points:
Striker (9) and withdrawn striker (10)
Force your opponent toward the flank.

Wingers (7 and 11)
Force your opponent toward the flank.

Midfielders (6 and 8)
Force your opponent onto his weaker foot.

Success moment:
10 1v1 challenges – two teams against each other – who wins the most challenges?

Training phase:
line training with 3 lines (6v7+GK)

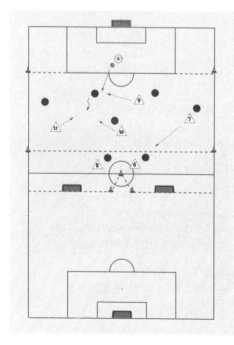

Organization:
- The 7 defenders can score
  - by crossing one of the two imaginary lines of the triangle with the ball
  - by playing the ball into one of the empty goals from the zone
- The 6 attackers and midfielders can score in the large goal.
- The goalkeeper cannot score.

Coaching points:
The midfielders must push forward in support to prevent a long ball from being played.

Striker (9)
Force the central defender toward the flank. Try to prevent the opposing team from playing the ball past you.

Withdrawn striker (10)
Pick up the defensive midfielder.

Winger (7)
Force your opponent toward the flank

Winger (11)
Squeeze toward the flank where the ball is.

Midfielders (6 and 8)
Pick up your direct opponent. Cover each other.

Success moment:
A goal scored after one of the defenders loses the ball counts double.

Game phase:
8v8 (depending on the number of available players)

Session 4
Development objective of the session
Session 4: The match analysis shows that the players on the other flank do not squeeze toward the flank where the ball is often enough. We start in the discovery phase again with 1v1 with the players in their actual positions. We then switch to the same drill with 3 lines from the previous session. The drill is adapted to the soccer problem. We finish the session with a match-related drill (11v11) against another age group.

Discovery phase: 1v1 with players in their own positions

Training phase: Line training with 3 lines (6v7+GK)

Game phase: Match-related drill (11v11) against another age group

Content of the session
Discovery phase:
1v1 with players in their own positions

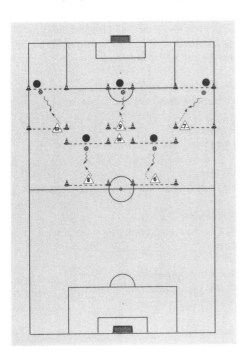

Organization:
Each player stands in a zone that corresponds to his match position.
- 1v1 with opponent
- Ensure that the players have sufficient pauses

Coaching points:
Striker (9) and withdrawn striker (10)
Force your opponent toward the flank.

Wingers (7 and 11)
Force your opponent toward the flank.

Midfielders (6 and 8)
Force your opponent onto his weaker foot.

Success moment:
10 1v1 challenges – two teams against each other – who wins the most challenges?

Training phase:
line training with 3 lines (6v7+GK)

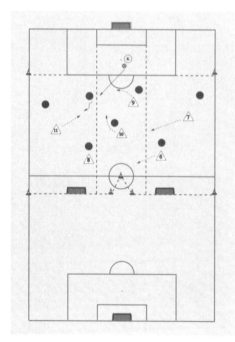

Organization:
- The 7 defenders can score
  - by crossing one of the two imaginary lines of the triangle with the ball
  - by playing the ball into one of the empty goals from the zone
- The 6 attackers and midfielders can score in the large goal.
- The goalkeeper cannot score.
- We have extended the edge of the goal area to the center line. When the players squeeze toward the other flank, they have to cross this line.

Coaching points:
The midfielders must push forward in support to prevent a long ball from being played.

Striker (9)
Force the central defender toward the flank. Try to prevent the opposing team from playing the ball past you.

Withdrawn striker (10)
Pick up the defensive midfielder.

Winger (7)
Force your opponent toward the flank

Winger (11)
Squeeze toward the flank where the ball is.

Midfielders (6 and 8)
Pick up your direct opponent. Cover each other.

Success moment:
A goal scored after one of the defenders loses the ball counts double.

Game phase:
8v8 (depending on the number of available players)

EVALUATION

Problem-oriented coaching

- *Have the players enjoyed themselves?*
  There was sufficient variation in the drills.

- *Has there been an influence on the soccer problem?*
  In real matches we saw good progress. The players were clearly influenced:

  - Pressing as a group was much improved.

- *Is the number of practice drills in the training sessions limited?*
  There are a maximum of 3 drills in each training session.

- *Is the number of practice drills in the module limited?*
  A total of 4 practice drills are integrated in the module. All other drills are based on these main drills.

- *Is there a good balance between match-related and non-match-related drills?*
  We only work with match-related drills. This follows logically from the soccer problem.

- *Is there a progressive buildup over a certain period?*
  Four training sessions are completed over a period of 3 weeks. The level of difficulty is slowly increased.

- *Are there sufficient repetitions for the players?*
  All players have sufficient repetitions.

- *Is sufficient consideration given to the age group of the players?*
  The drills used in these practical examples are oriented to the players' age group. The content is adjusted to the age of the players.

- *Are the drills adjusted to their level?*
  The drills are applicable at the highest level. If they are too difficult, the coach can easily adjust them.

- *Do the players have sufficient freedom of movement?*
  There are sufficient free moments for the players.

Practice Drills

1 v 1

Duel: 1+GK v 1
Opponent in front

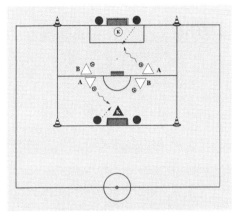

Be sure to maintain a good work/rest ratio.

Development objective
Training for 1v1 situations with opponent in front.

Organization
- Player A runs with the ball at the defender.
- Player B then runs with the ball at the defender.
- The attacker can score in the large goal and the defender can score in the small goal.

Success moment
Attackers v defenders. Who is the first to score 5 goals?

Switching positions
The attacker switches with the defender after each duel. After 4 duels, A switches with B.

Coaching points
- Cooperation between goalkeeper and defender.
- Knees bent, keep low.
- One foot forward. Push the attacker toward the flank.
- Stay on your feet.

Duel: 1 v 1
Opponent in front

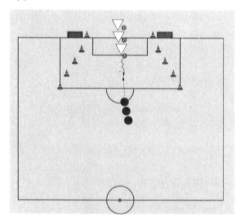

Depending on the level of skill of the players, the space can be made narrower or wider.

Development objective
Training for 1v1 situations with opponent in front.

Organization
- The player with the ball can score by crossing the line with the ball.
- The defender can score in either of the two nets.
- The further the attacker advances, the more space he has. The defender must challenge him as soon as possible and force him back.

Success moment
The attacker and the defender swap positions after the defender scores a goal.

Coaching points
- Try to challenge the attacker as soon as possible.
- Force him to use his weaker foot.
- Stay close to him if he moves backward.

Duel: 1 + K v 1
Opponent in front

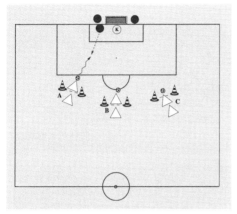

This drill is suitable for younger players
(up to age 12)

Development objective
Training for 1v1 situations with opponent in front.

Organization
- 3 permanent defenders and 6 attackers.
- After a successful attack, the attacker can move on to the next position.
- The attackers must take the ball past the defenders in one movement.

Success moment
Which players is the first to arrive back at his starting position? (For example, A – B – C and back to A.)

Coaching points
- Cooperation between goalkeeper and defender.
- Knees bent, keep low.
- One foot forward. Push the attacker toward the flank.
- Stay on your feet.

Duel: 1 + K v 1
Opponent behind

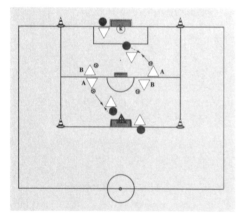

Let the player with the ball run with it (closer to real match situation).

Development objective
Training for 1v1 situations with opponent behind

Organization
- Player A plays the ball to the attacker with a defender behind him.
- Player B then plays the ball to the other attacker.

Switching positions
The player with the ball becomes the attacker and the attacker becomes the defender.

Success moment
The attackers must score 5 times within a given time.

Coaching points
- Try to get in front of your opponent.
- Don't commit a foul.
- Stay close to your direct opponent.

Duel: 1 + K v 1
Opponent behind

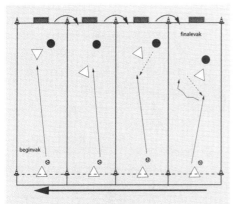

This drill can be used for other 1v1 situations.

Development objective
Training for 1v1 situations with opponent behind.

Organization
- Four zones are marked out.
- The ball is played to the attacker.
- 1v1 with the defender.
- The attacker can score in the small goal.
- The defender can score by crossing the imaginary line with the ball.

Switching positions
- The player who wins moves to the next zone.
- If the attacker wins, the defender remains in the zone.
- If the defender wins, the attacker stays in the zone and becomes the defender.
- The player who played the ball to the attacker becomes the attacker or the defender.
- The losing player in the final zone moves to the first zone.

Success Moment
Who is in the final zone after 7 duels?

Duel: 1 + K v 1
Opponent alongside

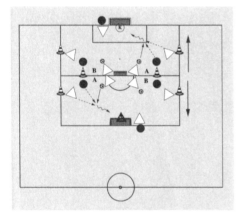

Depending on the strength of the defender, the attacker's cone can be positioned closer or further away.

Development objective
Training for 1v1 situations with opponent alongside.

Organization
The ball is played to the winger, who then goes 1v1 with the defender.

Switching positions
A becomes the defender, the defender becomes the flanker, the flanker takes over A's position.

Success moment
2-0 for the defenders. Can they keep their lead for 8 minutes?

Coaching points
- Don't dive in.
- A tackle is a last resort.
- Don't let yourself be isolated.
- Use your weight.

Duel: 1 + K v 1
Opponent alongside

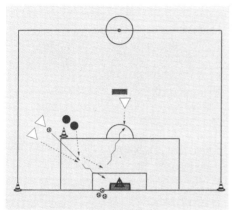

You can expand this drill to 2v2, 3v3 or 4v4. Enjoyment guaranteed!

Development objective
Training for 1v1 situations with opponent alongside.

Organization
- One attacker plays the ball forward to another attacker.
- The defender cuts across the run line and tries to win the ball.
- If the defender wins the ball, he turns back (or plays the ball back to the goalkeeper) and tries to score in the small goal. The second attacker tries to prevent this and to score in the large goal.
- If one of the attackers scores, we start again.

Coaching points
- Don't dive in.
- A tackle is a last resort.
- Don't let yourself be cut off.
- Use your weight.

1v1 circuit

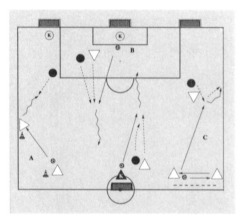

Tip: Be sure to maintain a good work/rest ratio.

Development objective
Training for various 1v1 situations.

Organization
3 groups of players – after 10 minutes they switch places.

A) Opponent in front
- The ball is played to the winger: 1v1.
- The attacker can score in the big goal (with or without a goalkeeper).
- The defender scores by passing the ball to the player who makes the initial pass to the winger.

B) Opponent alongside
- Two goalkeepers play the ball in: 1v1 with defender.
- Attackers can score in the large goal, defenders in the small goal.

C) Opponent behind
Two players pass to each other. One of the two plays the ball forward. 1v1 with defender follows. The attacker can score in the big goal. The defender can score by crossing the line with the ball.

Coaching points
A) Don't dive in.
Knees bent. Keep low.

B) Try to cut off your opponent's pass line.
Use your body as a block.

C) Choose the right moment to get in front of your opponent.

1 v 2

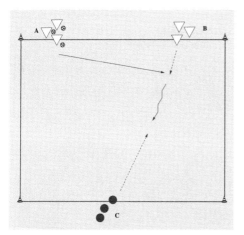

The chance that the defender will win the ball depends on his mental attitude.

Development objective
Defensive principles in situations where there is a numerical disadvantage.

Organization
- Both teams can score by crossing the line with the ball.
- If the ball goes out of play, dribble it back into play.
- Switch positions after a goal is scored.

Switching positions
A to B, B to C, C to A

Success moment
If the defender scores, the attackers have to carry out 10 push-ups.

Coaching points
- Mental attitude is important.
- Try to isolate the player who has the ball.
- Don't allow the opposition to play the ball past you too easily.

1 + K v 2

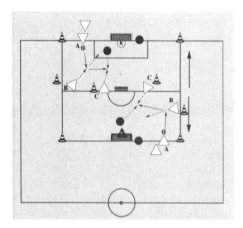

This drill can be expanded to 1v1, 2v2, 2v3 and 3v3.

Development objective
Cooperation between goalkeeper and defender.

Organization
Start with passing and shooting.
A plays the ball to B, B plays the ball to C.
After the ball is played to C, we play 1+Goal-keeper v 2 (= B and C).

Success moment
If the defenders score 3 times, switch positions.

Coaching points
- Cooperate with the goalkeeper.
- Stand off the two attackers, covering them both. Let the attackers make the choice.

2 v 2

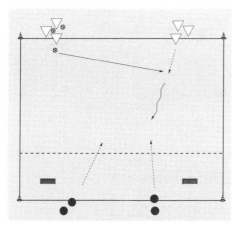

Coach indirectly too; motivate the attackers to take the ball past the defenders.

Development objective
Defensive principles

Organization
- If the defenders win the ball in the opposing team's half and cross the line (1) with the ball, the defenders become attackers.
- If the attackers score in one of the small goals (beyond the imaginary line 2) they remain as attackers.

Success moment
If one of the attacking pairs scores 5 times, the other players have to run once round the field.

Coaching points
- Cover each other (help).
- Communicate with each other.
- Don't run backward.

2 + K v 2 + K

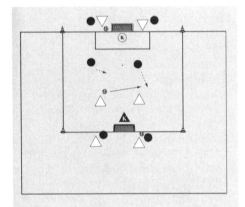

This drill can also be expanded to 3v3 and 4v4.

Development objective
Defensive principles

Organization
2v2
When a goal is scored, the players switch positions. The team that scores keeps the ball.
  - Ensure that plenty of balls are available around the field.
  - If the ball goes out of play, dribble it back into play.

Success moment
Which team is the first to score 5 times?

Coaching points
- Mark the player in possession closely.
- The other player provides cover.
- The last defender communicates with his teammate.

2 + GK v 3

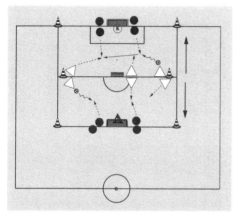

This drill is suitable for focusing on moving across toward the flank.

Development objective
Cooperation between goalkeeper and defender.

Organization
- The group of 3 can score in the large goal
- The group of 2 can score in the small goal.

Success moment
- When the defenders have scored 3 or 4 or 5 times, they become attackers.
- Each goal scored by the attackers is subtracted from the total (the attackers can reduce the score to 0).

Coaching points
- Try to cover each other.
- The last defender communicates with his teammate.
- Try to isolate the player who has the ball.

3 v 3

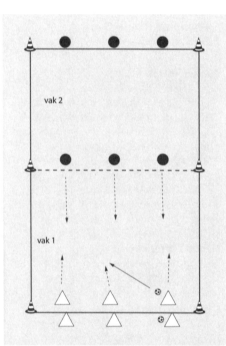

vak 2

vak 1

Let a fourth player pass the ball in to the attackers. This initiates an action and reaction sequence. The moment when the defenders exert pressure is closer to a real game situation.

3v3 is a very intensive, demanding drill. Be sure to maintain a good work/rest ratio.

Development objective
Coaching how to defend forward.

Organization
- *There are two groups of 3 in yellow vests and two groups of three in black vests.*
- *The two yellow groups have 6 opportunities (3 per group) to take the ball through the two zones.*
- *The yellow and black groups then swap roles.*
- *The defenders cannot enter the opposing group's zone until the ball is played in by the fourth player.*

Success moment
If the attackers take the ball through the first zone they score 1 point. If they take it through both zones they score 2 points. Who scores the most points?

Coaching points
- *Pressure the ball.*
- *Do not move back toward your own goal.*

3 v 3

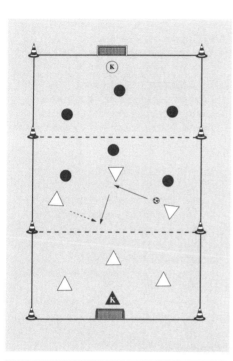

Development objective
Defensive principles

Organization
- 3v3 in the middle zone. When one of the teams succeeds in crossing the imaginary line into its attacking zone, it plays 3v3 against the defenders in the attacking zone.
- If the defenders in the attacking zone win the ball, they can pass to their teammates in the middle zone, who try to take the ball into their attacking zone.
- The drill is started again after a goal is scored.

Success moment
We play 3 x 10 minutes. One point is awarded per 10-minute spell.

Coaching points
- Force the attackers away from the goal.
- Push toward the flank where the ball is.

This drill can also be played as 2v2 or 4v4.

3 + GK v 4

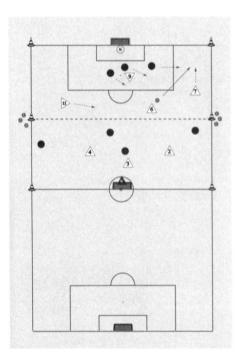

You set a time within which the attackers must score. They have to score with X minutes.

Ensure that there are enough balls available on the center line.

Development objective
Cooperation between the defenders and the goalkeeper in front of the goal.

Organization
- The four attackers start against the 3 defenders.
- The four attackers can score in the large goal, which is defended by a goalkeeper.
- The three attackers can immediately pass to one of their teammates in the other zone. We then have the same scenario in the other zone.

Success moment
Who is first to score 5 goals? When a team scores, the other team restarts in the direction of the other goal.

Coaching points
- Leave the widest attacker free when he has not got the ball.
- Mark closely on the flank where the ball is.

3 v 4

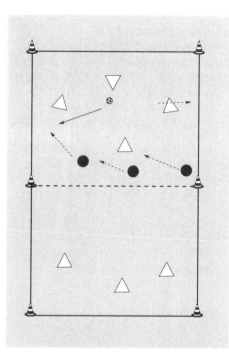

You can also use this drill with four defenders.

Development objective
Cooperation between the three defenders.

Organization
- Three defenders against four attackers.
- One of the four attackers tries to cross the imaginary line with the ball.
- If he succeeds he joins the players in the other zone.
- 3v4
- The three defenders turn around and defend in the other zone. The attackers have a limited time in which to cross the line (2 or 3 minutes).

Success moment
If the defenders prevent the attackers from crossing the line within the given time, they score one point. The attackers score one point each time they succeed in crossing the line.

Coaching points
- Move across toward the flank with the ball.
- Don't allow the opposing team to play the ball past you too easily.

4 v 4

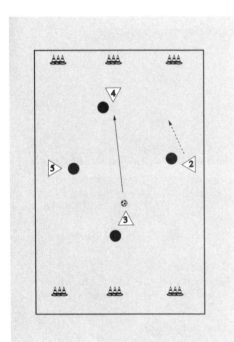

Development objective
Coaching the defensive principle of squeezing.

Organization
A point is scored by knocking a cone over with a shot.

Success moment
Who is the first to score 3 times (3 series). Who concedes the fewest goals in the 3 series.

Coaching points
- Keep pressuring the player – also when shooting at the cones.

4 v 5

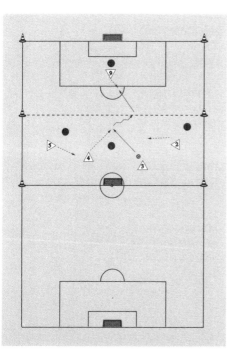

If it is too easy to pass the ball to the attacker, you can also make the attackers cross the imaginary line with the ball.

Development objective
Defensive principles.

Organization
- *3v4 in one zone*
- *1v1 in the other zone (striker and defender)*
- *The four defenders try to play the ball past the three defenders to the striker in the other zone (long forward pass).*
- *The three defenders try to make the playing area as small as possible and prevent the attackers from passing the ball forward.*
- *If the forward pass is successful, the players all join in and the zones no longer apply.*
- *When a goal is scored we start again.*

Success moment
Goals scored by the defenders before the forward pass can be made count double.

Coaching points
- *Keep pressuring the ball.*
- *Don't allow the opposing team to play the ball past you too easily.*

Game Drill (5v5)

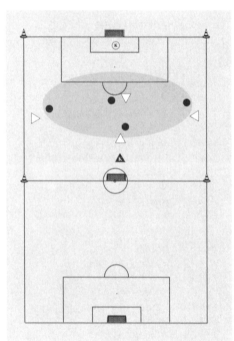

Development objective
Pressuring the opposition.

Organization
Field measuring 35 x 20 yards

Task
We leave player X relatively free and then pressure him when he receives the ball.

Success moment
Who is the first to score 5 goals? The winners can each shoot 5 times at the large goal defended by a goalkeeper.

Coaching points
- We exert pressure together.
- Don't allow the opposing team to play the ball past you too easily.

Line Training with 2 Lines

5 + GK v 6

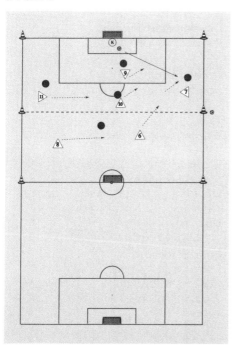

Development objective
Pressuring the opposition's build-up play.

Organization
- The group of six can score in the goal defended by the goalkeeper.
- The group of five can score in the empty goal.
- Wining the ball in the opposition's half scores 2 points, and winning the ball in the team's own half scores 1 point.

Success moment
Who is the first to score 6 goals?

Coaching points
- Close down space on the flank where the ball is.
- Force your opponent inside.
- Don't allow the opposing team to play the ball past you too easily.
- Keep pressuring the ball.

You can also reward play in the opposition's half by restricting the number of ball contacts in the team's own half.

6 v 6 + GK

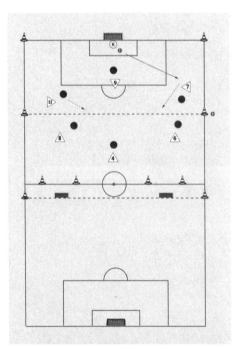

The gate can be widened or narrowed, depending on the level of skill of the players.

Development objective
Pressuring the opposition's build-up play.

Organization
- The players identified in the diagram by spheres are allowed two ball contacts in their own half. In the opposition's half they can play without restrictions.
- The "spheres" can score in the goal after first taking the ball through one of the two gates.
- The "triangles" can defend all over the field, also behind the imaginary lines.
- When the ball is back in the spheres' half, they must take it back over the imaginary line.
- The triangles can score in the large goal defended by the goalkeeper.

Success moment
All goals scored after winning the ball in the opposition's half count double. Who is the first to score 5 goals?

Coaching points
- Invite the goalkeeper to play the ball to a specific player.
- Close down the space on the flank where the ball is.
- Try to keep the opposing players in their own half.

6 + GK v 6 + GK

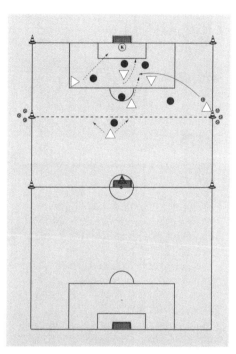

Development objective
The players' positioning for a cross in front of their own goal.

Organization
- We start the drill with a cross.
- Each second time that the ball goes out for a throw in, and each time a corner is conceded, the team in possession can cross the ball in front of the goal.

Success moment
A headed goal counts double.

Coaching points
- What position should the free man play?
- As the front man.
- In front of the opposition's best header of the ball.
- Make sure you stay in contact with the attacker.
- Don't let the attacker get in front of you.

Too little attention is generally paid to crosses in front of goal. A simple drill such as this compensates for this shortcoming.
- Put all the less gifted headers of the ball in the same team.

7 v 7

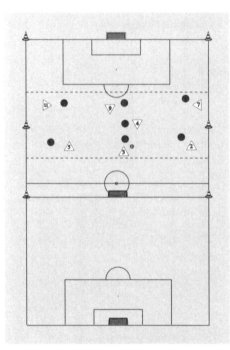

You can play this drill with or without goalkeepers.

Development objective
Cooperation between defenders and midfielders when the opposing team has possession.

Organization
- We play 7v7 in the middle zone.
- We can cross into the attacking zone by
  - running with the ball
  - playing a one-two passing combination
  - playing a forward pass

All the players can enter the attacking zone after the ball has been played into it.

Success moment
The team that scores first is awarded a 2-0 lead. We play for 25 minutes. Who wins?

Coaching points
- Keep the opposition away from the attacking zone.
- Force them toward the sideline.

Game Drill (8v8)

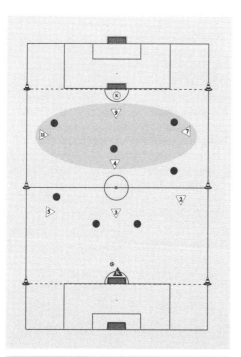

Development objective
Pressuring the opposition.

Task
Two-touch play in your own half; no restrictions in the opposition's half.

Success moment
Goals scored after winning the ball in the opposition's half count double.

Try to organize the game drill so that it as close to a real match as possible.

Line Training with 3 Lines

7 v 9 + GK

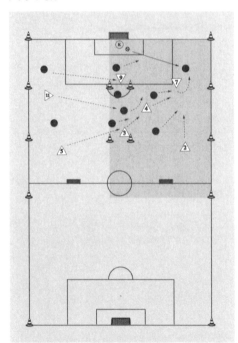

The drill is eminently suitable for giving the players practice in squeezing and for improving their positional play around the ball.

Development objective
Coaching defensive principles.

Organization
- *The goalkeeper has the ball and starts by playing it to the right or left back.*
- *If he plays the ball to the left back, we play in this zone up to the far post (shaded zone).*
- *The 9-man team tries to score in the empty goal.*
- *The 7-man team tries to win the ball.*
- *If the 7-man team succeeds in winning the ball and playing it out of the zone, we play back over the whole field.*
- *The 9-man team can score in the two empty goals and the seven-man team can score in the large goal defended by the goalkeeper.*
- *The above points apply similarly when the goalkeeper plays the ball to the right back.*

Success moment
The 7-man team is 2-0 in front. We have 20 minutes to play. The losers are responsible for cleaning up the equipment afterwards.

Coaching points
- *Keep pressing the ball.*
- *Leave the players furthest from the ball free.*

7 v 9

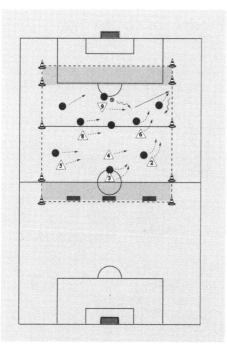

Development objective
Coaching defensive principles.

Organization
- *The 9-man team can score in one of the three small goals from the shaded zone.*
- *The 7-man team can score by playing the ball to a teammate in the imaginary zone. The offside rule applies.*

Success moment
The 7-man team is 2-0 in front.

Coaching points
- *Try to keep the opposition out of the zone.*
- *Play compactly.*
- *Close down the space on the flank where the ball is.*
- *Stay in contact with your opponent.*

Playing with three goals means that the central players get forward more. The zone can be made larger or smaller to suit the level of skill of the players.

8 + GK v 9 + GK

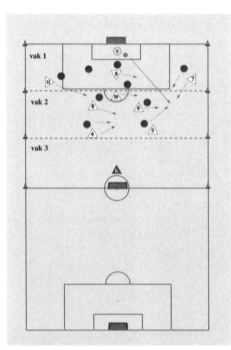

Development objective
Pressuring the opposition's build-up play.

Organization
- The field is divided into three zones.
If the 8-man team wins the ball:
   in zone 1 and scores = 3 points
   in zone 2 and scores = 2 points
   in zone 3 and scores = 1 point
- If the 9-man team scores in the large goal
   defended by a goalkeeper it is awarded 2
   points

Success moment
Who scores the most points in 15 minutes?

Coaching points
- Try to influence the build-up by leaving the
   weakest opponent free.
- Choose the right moment to challenge for
   the ball.

You can adjust the relative sizes of the zones. In the first phase, for example, you can make the first zone fairly large.

8 + GK v 9 + GK

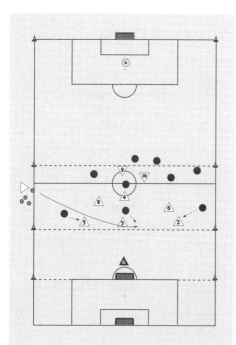

Development objective
Defensive principles for dealing with a cross, goal kick, etc.

Organization
When the ball goes out of play:
- *always restart with a goal kick by the goal-keeper*
- *always restart with a free kick*
- *always restart with a long ball forward*
- *always restart with a 1v1 on the flank*

Success moment
The team that scores the most goals wins.

Coaching points
- *Dependent on the chosen situation.*

Relatively little attention is paid to some aspects of soccer (defensive headers, position in front of goal, etc.). Starting with a cross or a corner gives an additional stimulus to some of these aspects.

7 v 10

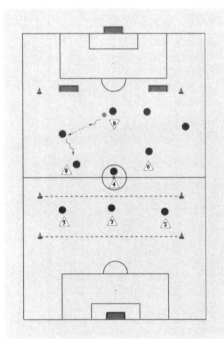

Development objective
Cooperation between midfielders and defenders.

Organization
- *The 10-man team has 5, 6, 7 or 8 x 3 min. to work the ball across the imaginary zone (rest period: 1 min 30 seconds).*
- *When they succeed, or if the 7-man team succeeds in scoring in one of the empty goals, we start again.*
- *The 7-man team can cancel out a success by the 10-man team by scoring.*

Success moment
The 10-man team has x chances. They keep score of how many times they succeed.

Coaching points
- *Play compactly*
- *Don't be tempted to dive in.*
- *Push toward the flank where the ball is.*
- *Try to stay out of the zone.*

9 v 10 + 2GK

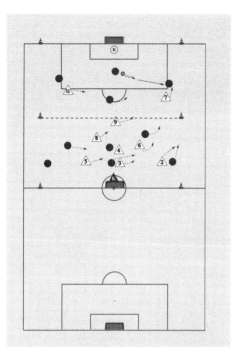

You can restrict the number of ball contacts of the 9-man team.

Development objective
Pressuring the opposition's build-up play.

Organization
- The 10-man team tries to keep possession.
- The 9-man team pressures them and tries to win the ball.
- The 9-man team can score in both goals.
- The 10-man team can score a point by playing the ball round x times.

Success moment
When the 9-man team scores 5 times, the teams switch.

Coaching points
- Do or don't pressure the goalkeeper?
- Choose the right moment.

9 + GK v 10

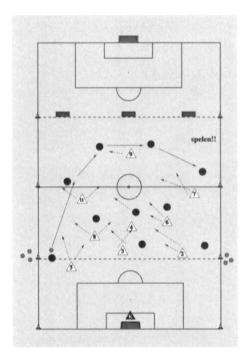

Development objective
Defensive principles.

Organization
- *The 10-man team starts with a passing and shooting drill on the left flank.*
- *When the left back has possession, the play becomes free.*
- *The players of the 9-man team adjust their positions to the position of the ball.*
- *When a goal is scored we start again, but now on the right flank.*

Success moment
The first team to score 5 goals wins.

Coaching points
- *Push toward the flank where the ball is.*
- *Play compactly.*
- *Communicate with the players in front of you.*

This drill is good for coaching positioning when the opposing team has possession. Other passing and shooting drills can are also possible of course.

10 v 10

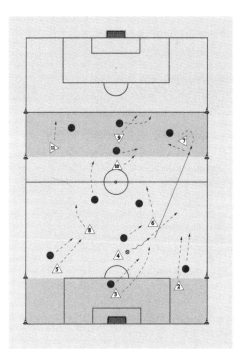

Development objective
Defensive principles.

Organization
- *Both teams play to retain possession.*
- *Each team has its own attacking zone.*
- *Each team tries to play the ball into its own attacking zone and then keep possession.*

Success moment
Which is the first team to play the ball round 5, 8 or 10 times in the attacking zone?

Coaching points
- *Keep the opposition out of the attacking zone.*
- *Defend forward.*

You can enlarge or shrink the attacking zones.

10 v 10

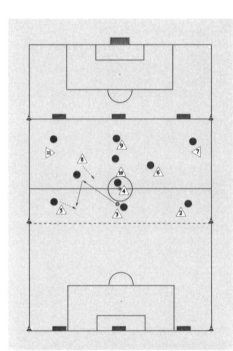

Development objective
Defensive principles.

Organization
- *The attackers try to score in one of the three small goals.*
- *The defenders try to win the ball and then play to keep possession.*
- *The duration of the drill is defined before hand (6, 7 or 8 minutes). When the time expires the players go to the other part of the field.*
- *The roles are then switched. The attackers become defenders and vice versa.*

Success moment
Which team has scored the most points after the drill has been carried out 6 times?

Coaching points
- *See defensive principles.*

This drill is good for coaching positioning when the opposing team has possession. Other passing and shooting drills can are also possible of course.

Game Drill (11v11)

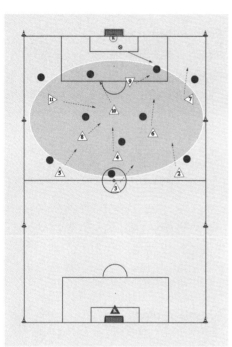

Development objective
Pressuring the opposing team's build-up play.

Task
Team A (1-4-4-2) plays defensively and tries to counterattack.
Team B (1-3-4-3) exerts pressure in the opposition's half and tries to score.

Success moment
Team X must score within a given period of time.

This is about exerting pressure in the opposition's half.

> Motivate the players. Enthusiasm is the basis for exerting pressure in the opposition's half.